More than

Penny Candy

More than

Penny Candy

Dolly Withrow

Elk River Press

Elk River Press
Charleston, WV 25301

Book and cover design:
John McKinnon, Silverhouse Design

Photograph location for the front and back cover
courtesy of The Strand

10 9 8 7 6 5 4 3 2 1

Printed in the United States of America.

Library of Congress Control Number:
2001093839

ISBN   0-9710389-0-2

Distributed by
Pictorial Histories Distribution
1416 Quarrier St.
Charleston, WV 25301

Table of Contents

PREFACE

One April evening in 1999, when nature had painted the West Virginia foliage lime green and streaked the sky with mother-of-pearl pink, I parked my car in a lot beside the Jackson County Board of Education. I then walked to a long line of yellow school buses where one driver welcomed me aboard. Having received permission to ride with the students, I rode for more than an hour to the end of the line where the last student departed for his short walk home.

I did not know it then, but that ride was the beginning of this book. After interviewing fellow travelers, I wrote the story about the long journey those students and others like them had to make to get to and from school. The next week, my article appeared in *The Jackson Herald*. A short time later, Mike Ruben, the publisher, asked me if I would write for *The Herald*. My first column was published in late May 1999, and that is how I became a weekly columnist. Almost all the essays in this book have been previously published in *The Jackson Herald*.

The topics are diverse and wide-ranging. I reordered the pieces, however, so that recollections of times past are at the start of the book. Most of the remaining essays are humorous reflections of times present. Many of you will identify with the small country store where I bought penny candy if I had any change after paying for groceries. Some of you will remember tent revivals and special grandparents and grade schools and summer magic that began on the last day of school. *More than Penny Candy* covers several childhood experiences in the 1940s and a few events and people from the '50s. More than three-fourths of the remaining book, though, comprises columns on today's society or on nature—on the behavior of both wildlife and on us humans.

There is something for readers of every age, but always, my intention has been to entertain first. On those rare days in my life as a writer, though, when I have heard that some of my work has enlightened and inspired as well, I am both humbled and gratified. No author could ask for more. It is an honor for me to find this avenue to share my writing with you, my reader. May you enjoy all the pieces of "Penny Candy." Whether the topics are sweet, tart, sticky, or hot, my hope is that you will devour and enjoy them all and share your thoughts about them with friends and family.

~Dolly Withrow

I. RECOLLECTIONS

Penny Candy

The store in which I bought penny candy when I was a child was little more than an unpainted shack. Tin signs advertising Coca-Cola, Mail Pouch tobacco, Lucky Strike cigarettes, and other products covered the front of the wide-boarded exterior. During hot weather, a squeaking screen door did little to keep out flies. As soon as I entered the rectangular building, I could hear the whir of a large fan that had been built into a lone window in the back wall. The intermingling smells of spicy lunch meat, cigarette smoke, and fresh fruits and vegetables gave the store part of its unique character. In late fall, the aroma of the gas heater announced the coming of winter.

The store's counter was L-shaped with the longer part facing the only door and the shorter counter running along the back of the narrow store. Shelves lined the long wall with canned goods. Treasures of penny candy lay just out of reach in the glassed-in counter. There were bee-bee bats, long twisted strands of licorice (some red, some black), bubble gum, and chewable wax figures filled with sweet-flavored liquids. I usually carried a tattered piece of folded notebook paper on which an order had been written. My reward for shopping was a nickel, which would buy a good variety of candies.

Clate and his sister, Mary Jane, were the owners. Mary Jane was a fixture in the store. With dark hair, curled tight to her head, and piercing brown eyes set deep in a chubby face like raisins punched into soft dough, she was an imposing figure to a small child. I remember her bright red nail polish with each pudgy finger boasting a long almond-shaped nail. I can still see her red polish reflecting the light from one of the naked light bulbs hanging from the ceiling. What I remember most about her, though, were the large diamonds she wore on the fingers of both hands, a fact that made me think she was wealthy. In retrospect, I know most of her wealth was tied up in those diamonds. She disposed of her duties in the manner of a professional.

Filling my order, she sliced lunch meat on a machine. Rhythmically back and forth went the large roll of meat as she pressed it against the circular rotating blade. Each slice fell onto a piece of waxed paper. When she shut the machine off, she tore a square of butcher's paper from a large roll. After wrapping the meat, she secured it with heavy white twine.

When it was time for me to choose my penny candy, I could never resist the wax figures. I chose the green because lime was my favorite. During the first few seconds the flavor—intense, sweet—burst free in my mouth. Soon, the wax was tasteless and had to be discarded. I was beginning to learn then that most good things in life are like that, short-lived.

After adding the prices of the items, Mary Jane announced the total. As I listened to the cha-ching of the cash register and the slamming of it metal drawer, I knew the transaction was almost over. During one trip in late fall, I was unable to buy candy because there was no change. On that cold autumn day, the trek up the steep hill through shadowed woods was long and burdensome. The penny candy remained out of reach, but it was such days that taught me other lessons. I learned early in life that some things would be forever out of reach and that I had to make the best out of the things I could have.

Many years after shopping in that little country grocery store, I have learned that most of what I enjoy has little to do with diamonds or wealth. Some of my greatest joys include love of family, a good book, and, yes, penny candy.

World War II

Sometimes all I could hear was the ticking of the mantel clock and the creaking of floorboards as Mrs. Mooney moved about in her kitchen preparing lemonade for our visit. Her smile, like a crescent moon tipping slightly upward on one side, brightened my childhood in the same way the slant of afternoon sunlight brightened her living room. I usually sat in one of two gooseneck rockers flanking her fireplace, and I breathed deeply so as to enjoy more fully the aroma of peanut-butter cookies baking in her oven. After she had entered the room and held in front of me the tray of cookies and a tall frosty glass of lemonade, she settled into the other rocker. Each week, I learned something about life from her.

The squeak of the rocker accenting her soft voice as she rocked back and forth, she often said, "Sometimes, Dolly, you just have to be patient. Tomorrow will get here, and you will look back on these days. You will remember them and know that everything happens for a reason."

She also taught me the thrill of learning new words. The first time I ever heard the word "boysenberry" was when she told me that she and her husband had managed to grow them in their back yard. She had made boysenberry preserves with their harvest, and she gave me a small jarful. I was about twelve years old when I began my weekly visits with Mrs. Mooney, and I looked forward to them the way hard workers look forward to quitting time.

She was already middle-aged when we began our fireside chats, and she was a lady in the real sense of the word. Wearing flowered dresses of ironed cotton, rimless glasses, and hair streaked with gray that she wore pulled to the back of her head in a bun, she was a devoted wife and homemaker. Never having worked outside the home, she kept her house immaculate, quiet, peaceful. It was a haven for a young girl who had long since learned to enjoy the company of adults. There was no generation gap in my family because I was an only child; adults and animals were often my only companions.

Mr. and Mrs. Mooney were for many years our next-door neighbors. After retirement, Mr. Mooney accepted a part-time job as an usher at a movie theater in downtown Charleston. During summers, he wore a white suit that sported a red carnation boutonniere.

One evening during the summer, as dark clouds rolled across the western sky, I stood looking wistfully toward the small Mooney house. That afternoon, I had knocked lightly at their front door but had received no answer. Cradling my white cat in my arms, I gazed toward their empty front porch. Then, I heard a door shut. Mrs. Mooney came out with a broom and began hurriedly sweeping her porch. I couldn't believe what else I saw. She wore a white short-sleeved tailored blouse underscored by—by what?—blue jeans. No!

Later, I learned she had heeded Uncle Sam's call. On every billboard I saw as I walked to Grandview School, there was the image of Uncle Sam, dressed in his top hat with his red, white, and blue uniform. He pointed a finger directly at me and beneath the picture was the caption: Uncle Sam Wants You.

Mrs. Mooney must have seen the billboards, too, because she answered the call by going to work at the Naval Ordnance Plant in South Charleston. For the first time in her life, she traded in her cotton print dresses for jeans. Our afternoon visits necessarily came to an end as all things do.

After all, during World War II, we each had a job to do. It was a time when Americans came together, disregarding differences rather than accentuating them. We had a common bond, and we Americans were one family. For that reason, we forged a strong nation. Each, in our own way, became a part of that generation Tom Brokaw has labeled "the greatest generation." On the home front, we worked to support our armed forces so that small countries being crushed under the heels of power-crazed dictators could regain their independence, their freedom.

I remember doing my small part by helping my grandfather hoe corn in his victory garden. I helped him carry buckets of water to the garden on sweltering sunlit days. We had no water hose, but we worked hard, and our garden was the talk of the neighborhood. My friends and I also peeled small sheets of tinfoil from gum wrappers.

We made large balls of tinfoil and contributed them to the war effort. We won the war and managed to keep our own independence, our own freedom. I sometimes wonder, though, if we lost a sense of duty to country, a sense of being one nation bound together by a common purpose.

I didn't know it then, but the loud ticking of Mrs. Mooney's mantel clock was speaking of time passage. It was ticking away the innocence of a nation, the end of yet another era.

Pocketful of Love

Growing up in a two-story stucco house with my mother, maternal grandparents, and various aunts and uncles, I had as companions mostly adults and animals. It was my grandmother, though, that provided the bedrock stability of my childhood.

Although the grass has grown on her grave for many years, she lives on in my memory. That is the way with loved ones; they don't completely die until there is no one left to remember them. My grandmother's death caused no great commotion in the universe as far as I know. Her permanent departure affected only a small number of her loved ones and friends. Yet, she was in many ways a remarkable woman, worthy of recognition she never received in her lifetime.

Wearing her gray hair wound into a circle at the top of her head like a silver crown, she moved about her old house with a regal dignity that belied her small income and simple homespun life. Industry, frugality, charity, and cleanliness—the kind that's next to Godliness—draw an accurate profile of Elmira Frame's character. She was the epitome of the Puritan work ethic. Work was her life. Even when she sat down to rest, she was snapping beans or making the long red curl of an apple peel fall into a small pan. She began each day in the kitchen where a round oak table with claw and ball feet sat in the center. I can still see her at her old-fashioned cabinet with its built-in flour bin. She made biscuits from scratch, kneading the flour, then rolling it to just the right thickness. She made brown gravy while huge biscuits baked. The two foods were generally our breakfast.

One morning, I heard my grandmother scream. I looked in time to see the long sleeve of her dress on fire. She had reached to a back burner on the gas cook stove and the front burner caught her sleeve on fire. Somehow, the flames were extinguished, but I remember accompanying her to the doctor because her arm had been badly burned. After returning home, she continued to work, never once complaining about pain or the inconvenience of an injured arm.

If, in the evening, she was too tired to work, she read her Bible, holding it just inches from her face. Cataracts had rendered her nearly blind, and yet her perception enabled her to see things that most people never noticed.

As time passed and we both grew older, I began to understand just how little she had either to use or to save. In retrospect, I still marvel at her ability to manage her income so that there was always a little tucked away for emergencies. Despite her failing eyesight, she made all her own clothes and sewed them by hand. Tiny stitches secured a large pocket to the front of each one of her aprons. And every morning, she filled that pocket with a variety of treasures taken from beneath her pillow.

I was never privy at any one time to the entire contents of that pocket. But I can still remember her hand reaching into that magical cloth well to retrieve a black leather change purse, which she opened to fulfill my request for a dime or quarter. I can still hear the snap of her purse when she closed it after handing me a coin. Whenever my childish heart was broken or my knee was skinned, she would again reach into her bulging pocket and pull out a bit of happiness in the form of candy or gum. She was, though, always able to distinguish between my need and my greed. When I asked for a second stick of gum, she would admonish me, saying that I must learn "to use a little and save a little."

Her managerial skills, although astounding, were confined to the boundaries of her house and yard. She lived in an era when a woman's place was definitely in the home. She accepted that most of the time, although occasionally I saw a dreamy, faraway look in her faded brown eyes. Nevertheless, her feet remained on practical ground, for she was a product of her times. Still, she had something special—something that would transcend death, live beyond the grave, and endure through the ages. My grandmother had a pocketful of love.

Prayer and Faith Tabernacle

Standing on the crest of Brickyard Hill, the Prayer and Faith Tabernacle with its yellow building blocks formed a rectangular structure that overlooked West Washington Street. The church was located about midway between my home and Sattes Cemetery where our family plot held only one member, my mother's sister, Aunt Inez Jane. Five other grave sites waited silently for death to fill them. I didn't know it at the time, but there was a common thread that ran through the tabernacle and Sattes Cemetery and the Frame household. It was all about living and dying and getting ready for dying, but I was too young and too engrossed in the day-to-day problems of a ten-year-old to understand anything about common threads.

The church was a place where sinners were often moved by the fire-and-brimstone sermons, followed by the usual hymns "Just as I Am" and "Bringing in the Sheaves." I sang with as robust a voice as I could muster. I noticed Mrs. Marcum's smile as she surely heard my voice rise above the others. Thinking her smile was one of approval, I sang even more loudly.

My words rang out like church bells themselves. "Bringing in the sheets, bringing in the sheets. We shall come rejoicing, bringing in the sheets." I wasn't sure what that song had to do with folks coming forward to the altar to be saved, but I could understand the rejoicing while bringing in the sheets, especially on cold winter days. I had helped my mother and grandmother take them off the clothesline after the icy wind had blown them cold and stiff. To be sure, getting them into the warm house was something to rejoice about.

During revival meetings at the church, some of the saved were led by the Lord to approach sinners as they stood with heads bowed (I thought hoping to be unnoticed) while the congregation continued to sing softly the words of "Just As I Am." Church members pleaded with sinners to come forward, to give their hearts to the Lord Jesus. Sometimes, those who believed would pull on the sinners' arms, nudging the reluctant toward the altar. The saved didn't want the sinner's souls to burn in the eternal flames of hell. Many nonbelievers, certainly fearful of such perpetual punishment, came forward and knelt at one of two oak altars in front of the church. There, they prayed with the saved and sanctified until they prayed through to salvation. It was not sufficient in the tabernacle just to be saved. One had to return to the altar for sanctification. Getting saved, then, was only the first step on the straight and narrow path to heaven's door.

Along with my childhood friends—Barbara, Rosie, Erma, and Georgie—I watched in awe during many services as the sinners and saved knelt around the altars. Their praying in unison became louder and louder until first one then the other prayed through to salvation. They had felt the Lord's spirit. Getting salvation was a glorious experience because it was not long until some of the members began to run up and down the aisles as they shouted, "Hallelujah, praise the Lord." "Amen" echoed throughout the congregation. I watched as both men and women brought forth white handkerchiefs, removed eye glasses, and wiped away tears of joy.

Mrs. Marcum and Mrs. Hill always got blessed. Mrs. Marcum was a middle-aged woman who wore her hair, as all women in the church did, pulled to the back of her head and twisted into a tight bun. She had naturally curly hair that was a mixture of blond and gray. It was difficult for her to look anything but pretty, try as she might. She wore rimless glasses that shone under the soft ceiling lights. No woman of any age was allowed to wear makeup, and all the women wore long-sleeved dresses, or at least dresses with sleeves that covered the elbows. Mrs. Marcum was a Christian who obeyed the Lord's commandments and followed every rule as far as I knew. She carried her large black Bible wherever she went, and it was well worn.

She always sat on the end of a wooden pew in about the fourth row from the front. As each service gained momentum, she began to shout in her seat. Then, she'd wave her snowy white handkerchief high over her head, making little circles in the air. My friends and I sat on the front row. When we girls heard the first "praise the Lord," we whipped our heads around to catch every shout, every movement. Erma or Barbara would gouge me in the ribs and whisper, "Look, Mrs. Marcum is going to get happy."

We knew when Mrs. Marcum's white hankie began to circle the air like a live halo moving above her head, it wouldn't be long before she'd be out of that seat and running up and down, up and down those aisles, followed quickly by Mrs. Hill. Middle-aged or not, those two ladies ran around the church like young gazelles. We watched with the utmost fascination, not at all understanding the full meaning of the soul's salvation or the accompanying shouts.

Nonetheless, I do remember that dwelling in a far corner of my heart—even in those green, naïve days—was a flicker of hope that their complete faith in some all-powerful being was well-placed. I envied their unquestioning faith, and I, too, wanted to believe that there was something greater and wiser and more powerful than we humans, some Being who would look over us, who had the power to heal my Aunt Sissy from her cancer, to stop her horrible pain. Sometimes, I prayed silent prayers while watching the shouters run the aisles. My prayers were simple, not much really, but they were from the sincere heart of a ten-year-old. I did believe that the church members believed, and that for me was good. It was a bit of sunshine in a young world filled with shadows and fears. I was glad to be in a place full of promise, a place where people held in their hearts a belief in goodness and forgiveness and salvation, although I wasn't sure then what salvation meant.

Before the next year would end, Sattes Cemetery would hold one more family member. In time, I would begin to sense the ghost of a thread that connected the cemetery, the tabernacle, and the Frame household.

Tent Revival

In the early 1940s, spring was announced in our neighborhood by the chirping of robins and the rhythmic pounding of stakes in the ground at the foot of our hill. In the large field, church members then stretched a tent from stake to stake. The canvas shelter would house a revival that some-times lasted for as long as two weeks if things went well. The success depended on the number of sheaves brought to the Lord.

Inside, wooden chairs were unfolded and placed in long rows, one behind the other, on each side of a wide aisle—an aisle carpeted by weeds and grass that had given way to a push lawn mower, the kind that needed no gasoline. In front, an elevated platform held a pulpit and a few additional chairs for featured singers and special guests. A portable generator provided power for a public address system and light bulbs that were strung at strategic places both inside and outside the tent.

The lights lured hungry mosquitoes looking for sustenance in human flesh. The revival drew people hoping to transcend the weakness of the human flesh. On warm star-sprinkled nights in early June, my friends and I would walk down the hill to the revival.

In retrospect, I wonder if I ever attended one of those revivals with the infamous Charles Manson. He and Sarah Jane Moore, also infamous because of her attempt to assassinate former President Gerald Ford, grew up in our general neighborhood. Sarah Jane attended Stonewall Jackson High School with me and was studious, taking part in many of the extra-curricular activities. I never saw her, though, at one of our late spring revivals.

During the June before I turned twelve, I listened intently as the preacher talked about the age of accountability. He wore shiny glasses. His bald head perspired, and always he stopped long enough to wipe away the beads of moisture with his white handkerchief. At some point each evening, he removed his dark blue suit jacket and rolled up his shirtsleeves. He leaned over the pulpit and pounded it with his fist to drive home his message. Of course, my friends and I knew we were the targets of his sermons, and we stared with wide-eyed wonder as he told us about death. He said that it might come like a thief in the night whether we were ready or not. Clearly, I was one of those dangling by a thread over Satan's fires.

One night, as I walked up the narrow pot-holed path toward home, often stumbling over large rocks, I vowed I would believe. The preacher said I could be saved in the twinkling of an eye, and so on that clear June night, I decided to never wear lipstick again. That would be my outward symbol of my inner belief; that was my promise, my part of the bargain. I was eleven years old when I tossed my tube of lipstick over the hill, where after more than half a century, remnants may still be there deep in the earth. We had been taught that the wearing of makeup was sinful, vain. In my heart, I knew I had done the right thing, and it seemed that the stars overhead took on a new brilliance. The stillness held a kind of holiness on that clear June night. I was suddenly so elated that I fairly floated the rest of the way home. At eleven, I was a mere child, and it was not long before I broke my promise and was wearing lipstick again. Guilt did not descend on me. Reasoning that God understood, I knew He worked in mysterious ways, for I had heard that many times.

Since then, I have learned that what I wear on my face is not as important as what I harbor in the deep recesses of my heart. Just as the true character of each spring revival was found inside that tent, the true character of each person is found, not on the outside, but deep inside the human heart. I have more compassion for people, for animals, for the human condition than I did at eleven when for a brief time I wore no lipstick.

On that star-scattered night, I was but a naïve child. In time, I learned that outward appearances are surface appearances. The human heart is where character and beliefs are stored. After all, it is the spirit, the soul, which will endure. All else is temporary.

Grandview Grade School

My first work of fiction was created at Grandview Grade School in the early '40s. A symmetrical red brick structure, the school in North Charleston, West Virginia, held grades one through six. The yard, surrounded by a chain-link fence, revealed mostly bare dirt interspersed with gravels. A narrow border of grass surrounded the edges like wisps of hair on a balding man's head. A no-nonsense concrete walk drew a straight line from the wide metal gate to the double oak doors.

The boys were restricted to one side of the walk where they played games such as marbles and mumblety-peg. The latter game was played with penknives the students routinely brought to school. The knives were thrown to the ground, and if the point of the blade stuck in the dirt, points were scored. Each boy carried his knife in a flapped pocket on the outside of one of his boots, the flap having been made especially for carrying penknives. As far as I know, no one was ever injured with the weapons the boys were allowed to bring to school. The boots were usually topped with corduroy knickers that made swishing sounds when the student walked down the hall.

Unlike the girls, the boys settled their quarrels swiftly with rough-and-tumble scuffles on the ground as onlookers gathered around and cheered. Teachers, who generally did not lead children in organized games, stopped the fights and issued doses of punishment to suit the offense. Teachers were free to issue just about any punishment they wished, a fact of which students were keenly aware.

On the other side of the walk, we girls enjoyed teeter-totters, chinning bars, swings, and various games that were played under the few trees at the edge of the yard. We seldom settled our disputes quickly. Our disagreements had a way of festering and lingering as the insiders held court in closed circles with their backs aimed at the targeted offender, or the outsider of the moment. Girls whispered and snickered and sometimes chanted nasty rhymes. I suppose there have been insiders and outsiders on school grounds for as long as there have been schools.

At the beginning of each day's classes, a loud bell rang, and we filed silently into the building. Inside, wide oak steps led from a large entry hall up to the second floor where the principal's office and upper-grade classrooms were located.

I remember the first-grade room with its musty cloakroom that held winter galoshes lined up under red and black checkered jackets. Girls' leggings, matching coats, and toboggans, smelly with melted snow, hung around the walls on large hooks. The school reeked of paste and crayons and purple gelatin from the hectograph Miss Rhodes, our teacher, used for reproducing pictures and words.

Before the first lesson began, we stood beside our small wooden desks, bowed our heads and recited the Lord's Prayer. After the soft "Amens," we pledged allegiance to the American flag, which was located in the front of the room and just under a large portrait of George Washington, who we were taught was the father of our country. A belief was instilled in us then that there was an entity greater than we humans, that we were not the center of the universe, and that belief created in most of us a set of values that has continued to cling like a second skin throughout our lives.

The school administrators were concerned about our health, and those of us who were frail-looking had to form long lines down the hall. We brought our tablespoons from home and at the white porcelain water fountain, we were each forced to swallow a spoonful of cod liver oil. As far as I know, we weren't harmed much, but I doubt if we were helped much either. Mental nutrition was the key to our success, though, and my world was about to expand.

Bells should have rung, stars should have come out at noon and the sun at night because another wonder was occurring. I was learning how to read. As is true with most people, however, for many years I thought little of my newly acquired skill. I never thought that somewhere along the way a patient teacher had prodded and probed and repeated until I began to understand that the mixing and mingling of letters created words that, in turn, created sentences. Doors to new worlds opened to me, and I began to read everything I could find. A short time later, I was taught to write, a skill that would open many more doors.

None of our teachers used terms like *self-esteem*, and in retrospect, I don't think they gave a tinker's dam about our self-esteem, at least not directly. I believe they knew that if we learned, our self-esteem would take care of itself. They cared very much about our learning, and they were strict on anyone who disrupted the class. That was simply not tolerated, so the days were long and tedious in those first few years of school. We learned to endure, and we learned to learn. There were no shortcuts, no easy steps. We had to memorize some facts and reason out others. We had no choice. We had never heard of social promotions. If we failed, we failed, and our failings were our fault—not society's, not our teachers', not our parents', but ours and ours alone. There were no grants for us, and no excuses were offered for our failings. We knew, maybe instinctively, that if we didn't learn the material, we would live (in most cases, continue to live) hardscrabble lives. Getting an education—a real education—meant we could really read and write and count. Only then could each of us have a chance at a life that was a step up from the lives of our parents.

Since we had few purchased games or toys, we learned early on to be creative. Such creativity came in handy when teachers distributed surveys with strange questions. How many bedrooms are in your home? What did you eat for breakfast? Do you have a private bedroom? Do you have a refrigerator in your home?

Since I was embarrassed to tell the truth, I created one of the most affluent homes in the community. I had a large bedroom of my own, (one of six bedrooms in our hill mansion). My room boasted around-the-wall shelves laden with leather-bound books. We had a dozen or so radios, and my breakfasts were fit for a princess. Of course we had a refrigerator. How else could I have enjoyed such lavish breakfasts? It was then that I wrote my first work of fiction in Grandview Grade School.

Summer Magic

Nothing was sweeter than the last day of school, a day that ushered in the long hazy summer. As we ran through the double doors of Grandview, we chanted, "School's out. School's out. Teachers let the fools out." My friends and I, leaving the fourth-grade classroom for the last time, ran toward our homes on Brickyard Hill, toward a summer offering days that would line up one after another like pearls on a string. As is true with looking forward to a vacation, our anticipation of summer was usually greater than the summer itself. Still, we knew how to entertain ourselves.

We played the usual games: prisoner's base, red rover, hide 'n seek, hopscotch, school, and movie stars. Our imagination was our greatest toy, and we used it daily. We sometimes jumped rope and sang, "Down in the valley where the green grass grows, there sits Barbara as sweet as a rose. Along came Hayes and kissed her on the cheek. How many kisses did he give her?" We counted each jump, and the longer the endurance of the jumper, the more imaginary kisses she received. Giggles and red faces followed, for it was a different time. Blushes were frequent, and modesty was prevalent.

When we played school, I was the teacher—a mean one, too, I might add. One of our favorite pastimes, though, was playing movie stars. Sometimes, I was Dale Evans, and I traveled by horse alongside Roy as we fought the bad guys. It was a world of innocence when good always triumphed over evil. Other times, I was Betty Grable in a short glittery outfit, singing "Put Your Arms Around Me, Honey." We had heard that Grable's legs had been insured for a million dollars. Wow! That was the kind of news we liked to pass along. We knew she was a pin-up girl for the men serving in World War II, and that made her a super star.

Saturday afternoons were special, for that was when we sometimes had enough money to go to the movies. We walked down Brickyard Hill and up Washington Street and past Sattes Cemetery and finally arrived at the West Theater on Charleston's West Side. The theater was billed as Charleston's finest. There, we could spend an entire afternoon watching two movies, a serial (*Perils of Nyoka* comes to mind), cartoons, previews of coming attractions, and news of World War II. Popcorn was popped fresh, and an usher, using a flashlight, showed us to our seats. Since the reel ran continuously, we could enter the theater at any time. Movies expanded our small world and fed our imagination.

What I liked most about summers, though, were those times when my family and I, just before dark, sat on wooden benches in the shade of our front porch. We tried to escape the heat that had already pounded its way inside. On clear days, the evenings provided a view that extended beyond the dirt road in front of our house and down two hills, then across a hollow to a distant hill where trees rose to meet a scarlet sunset.

I remember watching my grandfather as he knocked the bowl of his pipe against the edge of the bench, readying the pipe for a refill. He pulled a small rectangular package of Cutty Pipe tobacco from his pocket, stuffed some in his pipe, then struck a large match on the stucco wall behind him. He put the fire over the fresh tobacco, and drew in the smoke, making a "pff" sound with each draw. In the evenings after the sun had slid behind the distant hill, I could see in the light of the flaming match his small round cheeks puffing in and out as he drew in the smoke. Burned from long hours he spent each day in his garden, his cheeks were as scarlet as the sunset.

Taking the pipe out of his mouth and jabbing it into the air toward us, as though reinforcing his point, he often said, "If man had been meant to fly, God would have give him wings." As young as I was, I knew that man was already flying and, somehow, I sensed that tomorrow would bring even more remarkable discoveries, more inventions, a different world.

Topics on our front porch changed as rapidly as designs in a kaleidoscope, and it wasn't long before I would enjoy yet another ghost story or hear about the time my Uncle Hobert was climbing up the hill and saw a man hanging by his neck from a tree limb. As my uncle approached the tree, the man disappeared. That, of course, was not a ghost story. That really happened. Then, there were times my grandfather told about fighting a huge black snake that stood on its tail and fought him. It was taller than my grandfather, who, in the middle of the mystical forest, always won the battle with the serpent. Each time I heard the story, I was relieved again at his winning. I believed every word of all the stories I heard on that porch, and to this day, I enjoy telling a good story in return. Summers, after all, are filled with the special magic of a child's world, and the last day of school is when the magic begins.

Sattes Cemetery

When my world was fresh and full of promise, when my friends and I could fly high over rooftops and emerald green hills, when we could be Captain Marvel, Superman, and movies stars, when anything was possible, Sattes Cemetery was a focal point in our lives.

At times, it was a place of sorrow as we said our farewells to a friend or family member. At other times, it was a place of entertainment as we sat on a large boulder that cantilevered precariously over Washington Street far below.

It was there that we talked about our dreams and hopes and plans for the future. The cemetery was also a place of mystery and fear as we walked to the graveyard and had to pass an empty, dilapidated house. We had heard that the man who had once lived happily in the deserted house had since committed suicide over his wife's grave. The rumor added to our sense of adventure since we were too young to understand the tragedies in true stories.

Sattes Cemetery provided more than entertainment and a final resting place for loved ones. It provided food for our table. I remember golden summer days when my mother and two aunts collected paring knives and pokes (brown paper bags for readers not born in West Virginia) and donned wide-brimmed straw hats that topped sun-lined faces and faded print dresses. Although I was no more than seven or eight, I was allowed to go green picking with them. Both the cemetery and the path leading to it offered the filet mignon of wild greens. There, we could find both creasy and poke greens.

It was during those times when my mother and aunts searched for food that I looked closely at Sattes. Some of the tombstones were large and impressive. Even in 1942, though, time had eroded the surfaces of letters on the stones, letters that at one time identified the dead in proud bas-relief. The names on many stones had disappeared altogether, just as the people themselves had disappeared from life and were necessarily fading from memories. Their disappearance would be final only when there was no one left on earth to remember them. A few graves had only small metal markers that had been provided free by local funeral homes and other businesses. The white cardboard inserts were blank, for the names written in ink had long since been obliterated by the wind and rain and snow and, yes, the unrelenting passage of time.

It was on Decoration Day each year that in our family plot the grave itself became the focus of our efforts. Aunt Sissy cut red, white, and pink roses from bushes in our side yard, wrapped them in wet newspapers, and carried them out the dusty road toward the cemetery. We also took a sickle and rake, along with a couple of Mason jars half-filled with water. In the cemetery, after we cleared Aunt Inez's grave of weeds, Aunt Sissy placed the roses in the water-filled jars, which she, in turn, placed on her sister's grave. It was on that day that we met other visitors who were paying respects to their deceased loved ones. Sattes, like most small country graveyards, contrasted sharply with the large manicured cemeteries of today. Families owning a plot had the freedom to do with their plots whatever they wished. Some plots were surrounded by metal fences. Others had white picket fences. Still others were marked simply by the border of grass surrounding them.

Today, Sattes Cemetery and the graves of the voiceless occupants are obscured by tall weeds and undergrowth. The road that once led to the cemetery has disappeared. To get to the graves today, descendants must climb a steep, weed-infested path.

Our collective remembering of those who have gone before us, our visiting ancestors' graves on each Memorial Day, our clearing of weeds and our offering of flowers (real or otherwise)—it is these acts that distinguish us as caring humans beings.

I no longer believe that anything is possible, for my fresh green world is now a world of graying experience. Still, I nurture a hope that one day we descendants can once again chat with others on a sunny Memorial Day when small American flags and red roses brighten the graves of those buried in Sattes, many of whom fought in wars to ensure the freedom we enjoy today.

Childhood Journey

Thousands of stars winked in the velvet void of a night sky in late summer. Sitting between my mother and my Aunt Sissy on the top concrete step of our front porch, I could see in the far distance countless other winking lights. From my young vantage point, they appeared to make up the whole of a large city—a city at once magical and mysterious.

Pointing toward them, I asked, "What is the name of that town where all those lights are burning?"

Aunt Sissy said, "That's not a town, honey. That's the Carbide plant."

I was not yet convinced and on clear nights during that vanishing ninth summer of my life, I continued to sit on our steps, gazing at those lights and dreaming of faraway places. Once each evening as I watched the tiny bright dots winking at me, I could hear—just barely hear—the wail of a lonely whistle as a train passed through the valley below the hill where we lived. I couldn't see the light of the train, but I could imagine its dark form as it roared past the houses and people rooted in place, unable to move beyond where they were. Passenger trains were plentiful then, and when the train passed through each evening, I wondered who was riding in it and where it was going. I dreamed of growing up and seeing the world. I thought traveling would make me wise. I was wrong, of course. Visiting exotic locations does not necessarily make us wise. Rather, it is the journey through life itself that gives us knowledge, insight. My family and I were about to travel through a difficult place.

The evenings gradually became too chilly for us to sit outside. The autumn leaves that had burst forth in their array of oranges and reds and golds soon fell to the icy ground. The dismal bark of tree limbs silhouetted against a bright blue winter sky looked like dark skeletons. As the nights grew ever colder, I noticed that my aunt grew thinner. Then, one morning, she did not get out of bed. Soon, she began to moan and talk of unbearable pain.

One day in early spring, the doctor came to our house and sitting outside on a wooden bench, he broke a dead branch from a nearby tree. With it he drew in the dusty earth a sketch of my aunt's female organs, illustrating for my family the extent of the cancer.

Shaking his head from side to side, he said softly, "I'm afraid it's too far gone."

During the summer, the preacher from Prayer and Faith Tabernacle came and asked my aunt if she wanted a healing service. She smiled weakly and said, "Yes."

Soon, the preacher returned with several church members. They knelt around her white iron bed and prayed aloud in unison. Then, the preacher placed oil from a small bottle on her forehead.

The next morning she arose and walked down the outside steps in the pale sunlight. She ate a large breakfast and later that day snapped green beans. For six months, well into the next autumn, she seemed to be healed. One day, though, she was back in bed and during each winter night of my eleventh year, I heard her pray for God to take her life. I'd place my hands over my ears to muffle her cries because her prayers broke my heart. She died the following spring, leaving an empty place that has never been filled.

That's the way hard journeys are, but they can also leave us stronger. No more could I run to Aunt Sissy with childish complaints. Just before my next birthday in late summer, I sat alone on the concrete step where my mother, aunt, and I had sat two years earlier. I looked at the stars sprinkled overhead and wondered if Aunt Sissy could see me. All sorts of folks think they have the answer to that. They don't. I looked at the Carbide lights, and I knew they did not make up a city, magical and mysterious. I had already traveled much of the world, but I had not gone far from our neighborhood.

After many years, I have come to realize that we can see the world in different ways. I once had a colleague who said that she divided people into two general categories: those who traveled and those who didn't. As an infrequent traveler, I knew into which group she had tossed me.

Since those days of yesteryear when my world was confined to those steps, that house, that small corner of earth, I have journeyed far from my childhood home. Many of my travels have been through realms of gold, through books, but most of what I have learned has been during life's journey under both dark skies and twinkling stars.

Childhood Ghosts

Driving on a skinny blacktop road in West Virginia, I passed farmhouses, spring gardens, and a line from which clothes billowed like colorful sails in a gentle breeze. I passed a hillside dotted with gravity-defying goats and pastures filled with grazing cattle. Soon, though, I was gliding over the interstate, traveling south toward my childhood home on Brickyard Hill.

It had been many years since I left the house where I grew up. A half-hour later, as I parked in front of the old two-story stucco house, I noticed cirrus clouds etching white feathers against a sky of palest blue. Despite the sun-washed hillside behind the house, I had a feeling as empty as the old home place itself. Gone were the concrete steps where on balmy summer evenings many years ago I had gazed at Carbide's lights and dreamed of faraway places. The steps on which I had sat with my mother and Aunt Sissy had been ripped from the front porch, leaving a gaping wound. The porch itself, although running the length of the house, seemed smaller than I remembered. A crack in its cement floor extended from one end to the other. Sealed with tar, the patch formed a long, jagged scar.

Before I was born, my maternal grandfather and two of his sons had built the house, digging out a clay bank into which our home would sit. Boasting a hip roof, it was a symmetrical structure with a center door downstairs and one up, each flanked by two windows. The covered porch upstairs provided protection for the one below where, throughout childhood, I sat and listened to adults talk about snakes and politics and neighbors and ghosts. It was on that porch that I learned the joy of listening to both tall tales and real-life stories. In retrospect, I know it was there that I, in turn, learned to tell stories.

I walked across the porch and peered through a downstairs window into a room that had served as both bedroom and living room when I was a child. It was now no more than a shadowed cavity, void of furniture, and it held ghosts of its original occupants. I could see my grandmother rocking by the fireplace and reading her Bible, holding it just inches from her face. I could see my red-cheeked grandfather lighting his pipe and telling yet another joke. I could see my Aunt Sissy, wearing a flowered print dress, her blue eyes looking at our white cat that purred contentedly on her lap.

My heart beat faster as I stared through the dusty windowpane. Alone, lonely, I backed away and walked up the outside steps to the porch behind the house. Littered with old cardboard boxes, broken trellises, and pieces of sharp glass, it also held ghosts of family members long dead. I could see my Uncle Alfred sitting on a wooden bench, his black hair catching the sun's rays as he leaned over to pick up his shotgun. I could see the patina of its warm polished wood as he squinted one eye shut to look through the gun barrel. I could see him pull a long metal rod through the barrel. A soft cloth was somehow attached to the rod so that it cleaned the inside of the barrel. He was readying his gun for a hunting trip. He would give up hunting in old age, for the closer he came to death, the more he respected life. I could see my Uncle Hobert giving his beagle a bath in a round zinc tub. As I stood there, I realized that only my mother and I are left to harbor memories of the old house and of the people who helped to mold the person I have become. My mom is eighty-nine, and as I walked to my car, my sense of mortality intensified.

Driving back home, I again drove over the blacktop road running alongside farmhouses and gardens, goats and cattle. On my way home to our country cottage, I left the past and returned to the present.

Back Roads of Christmases Past

Yellow flames dance among logs in our family-room fireplace, but wood does not feed the fire. Rather, burning gas creates the flames—gas provided by a company whose officials send us a monthly invoice and wisely hope for more cold weather. Made to look real, the logs are as false as the have-a-nice-day mantra repeated by strangers to strangers throughout the land. The beauty of our fireplace, though, is that we aren't forced to buy wood or cut trees or chop wood or carry out ashes. Artificiality does have its few saving advantages.

During each Christmas season, homes near and far are filled with made-in-China decorations. Outdoor electric lights brighten dark winter evenings as do indoor plastic candles (also powered by electricity). Using decorations, the source of which we don't examine too closely, we somehow produce an unsettling magic.

I look at the miniature wonderland I've created for our three grandsons, or so I tell myself. A four-foot tree of plastic stands in the center of an antique library table. Colored wooden beads form a bright garland, and wooden clothespins, painted like toy soldiers, march around the bottom branches. As in the real world, my make-believe world permits the genuine to ride uneasily alongside the artificial.

On the back of each soldier's red jacket is written in crudely painted white letters, "LaPlace '68." Real memories surface. I see our two rosy-cheeked children sitting at a tan Formica-topped table in our Louisiana home. I see them transforming clothespins into snappily dressed soldiers. Those special ornaments have adorned each of our trees since that Southern winter of 1968. The ornaments are as genuine as the memories. Our son and daughter now have children of their own. Our daughter's two sons, Matt and Andy, have already helped her to create soldiers from clothespins that now march around her tree.

Providing the focal point of our village, the tree is laden with ornaments, each of which tells its own story of Christmases past. Beneath the tree, cotton emulates snow. Books stacked high under the cotton form snow-covered hills on which are perched small churches and houses overlooking a pond with skaters. A diminutive restaurant with a mullioned window reveals inside a well-lighted dining room where tiny people sit around a table with their bowed heads and steepled hands. The whole scene, as plastic as any scene can be, nonetheless provides a strange kind of holiday cheer. It offers an imitation Norman Rockwell village where cares and heartaches and pains do not exist. To be sure, this world of pretense is a child's world on one level. On quite another, though, this wee wonderland is a place where weary adults at the end of long days can let their eyes twinkle in the glow of tiny lights, where they can for a brief time let their memories wrap around the back roads of times past, where they can pull from those memories the best, the funniest, the most poignant of past seasons.

As Bill, my husband, and I sat near our magic village recently, he shared with me memories of several childhood Christmases. When he and Jim, one of his friends, were about twelve or thirteen, they hunted the snow-covered hills near their Dunbar, West Virginia, homes for two beautiful Christmas trees, one for each. Separating, the boys circled the hills in opposite directions. It was not an easy search because jutting out of the clay soil were mostly scrub pines. They were plentiful. Each of the three years, Bill would have little luck and finally would give up and cut a scraggly pine. Disappointed, he would drag his Charlie Brown tree down the hill. Smiling broadly, Jim soon followed. Making a wide path in the snow behind Jim was a beautiful spruce—the perfect tree.

It was not until several years later, after Jim had served in the para-troopers during the Korean War, that Bill discovered where Jim had found his perfect tree year after year. During each trip, he would go to the top of the hill where a small country cemetery boasted symmetrical spruce trees. There, Jim climbed almost to the top of a big spruce. Once anchored firmly to the tree, he would saw off the top and drag home the ideal tree. Those are the kinds of memories that villages and dancing flames amid artificial logs evoke. While those trappings are artificial, they trigger memories of friends and times long gone—memories as genuine and homegrown as the decorations were then.

Picture This

Sitting at our dining room table, I look beyond a small pass-through to the kitchen where double windows reveal a slate-gray November morning. A steady rain launches even more fall leaves; they float earthward. Nature's cycle continues, grounding me in reality.

Undoubtedly a collectible and perhaps even an antique, a reverse painting-on-glass pulls at my attention. It hangs on the wall facing me.

Surrounded by a three-inch ornate frame, the painting itself is no more than 20 inches wide and 16 inches tall, but it reveals to me a story about life. I gaze at the country scene with a lake on the left. A sailboat glides over still waters. To the right, a farmhouse sits atop a small bank. The house boasts windows that exude a subtle light, a light with the same softness as that in the small room where I sit. The unknown artist, surely long dead, has used mother-of-pearl to illuminate the windows in the two-story house.

In this room, on this morning filled with fog and mist, I am surrounded by paintings and crystal and Fenton glassware and even a set of depression-glass dishes, all of which have been handed down to me and my husband by family members who have passed away (a euphemism we use for died). The chilling realization I experience is that our possessions usually outlive us, an irony that seems unfair. Then, I realize yet again that we never really own anything—not land, not houses, not things.

The painting that graces the wall beyond the maple table where I sit belonged to my mother-in-law. For many years, it was at home on her knotty pine wall where I thought in my younger days it would forever remain. I know now that although we thought of it as her picture, she really had it only on lease, so to speak, for the time she was on earth. That picture, like everything we think we own, we don't. The landscape with its mother-of-pearl enlightenment hangs ever so temporarily in our home now. One day, like the fall leaves themselves, it will be cycled downward to our offspring, where it will find yet another home, which, in turn, will also be temporary.

Most of us know or have known people who have spent much of their lives fighting over a few feet of land, over boundaries, over property lines. They battle neighbors over fences and in court. In general, they make their own lives miserable and all because of land they can use only as long as they live. In William Faulkner's *The Sound and the Fury*, a 33-year-old "idiot" is cheated out of his inheritance (his land), but he is never unhappy. After his relatives sell his land, he enjoys watching the small white golf balls fly through the air as golfers hit them from hole to hole on the land that has been transformed into a golf course. The idiot seems to have wisdom we cannot comprehend. The other family members, rich with money from the idiot's land, remain discontented.

My mother-in-law came to a realization before her death that her earthly possessions were of no more use to her. Frail and fragile, she moved in with her daughter and a year or so later asked her son and daughter to divide her possessions, to take what they wanted, to give them a place in their home.

The picture reminds me of my mother-in-law, Ora Withrow, who knew how to transform a house into a home, into a place where we were always welcome. I remember especially Thanksgiving at my mother-in-law's home. The crystal that now sits on a shelf in my dining room graced her table on holidays. I remember Thanksgivings in her home. Mouth-watering aromas of baked turkey, dressing, and her special macaroni casserole filled the house. Her macaroni was a traditional dish, served every Thanksgiving and Christmas. I watched her each year as she mixed the ingredients, until I can now make a fair facsimile of her recipe. Her mother had made the dish when she was a child. She handed down the recipe to Ora, and now I prepare it each year. I know that one day my daughter will continue the tradition. The reverse painting-on-glass reminds me on this misty November morning of all the good times we had on those special holidays.

The glass painting reminds me of something else. As long as we remember our ancestors and remember others whom we have loved but who live no more, they nonetheless live on. They live in our hearts and in our memories. Perhaps, after all, that is one reason our possessions outlive us. They remind the living of times past, of events that might otherwise be forever forgotten. Outside, sun has transformed the grayness into a golden morning.

End of an Era

A slight-built man with graying blond hair and teasing blue eyes, he was a carpenter by trade. Through more than half a century, he provided for his family by spending hot, melting days installing roofs on houses after he helped to build the frame that held them. Inside, he plied his construction skills to everything from partitions to shelves to cabinets. At home, he built tables, benches, and china cabinets for his wife's lifelong accumulation of dishes and crystal. Indeed, he had built the house in which they lived, although he added rooms and changed porches and moved rooms, creating a kitchen upstairs where once a bedroom stood. The kitchen became part of the warm heart of his home.

In the evening of his life, he filled customers' requests by constructing gun cabinets in a small room adjoining the basement of his home. There, he had organized the tools of his trade. Around the walls surrounding his worktable hung screwdrivers of various sizes, small saws, hammers—all the necessary implements for carpentry work.

More than half a century earlier, on June 15, 1929, he married his sweetheart, Ora Frances Thomas, who on that day became Mrs. Howard Wilson Withrow. During the Great Depression, the couple had few possessions, but their love for each other gave them the greatest gift of all, a marriage that lasted almost sixty years.

For better or worse had meaning for them, and they would experience times both better and worse. Their marriage produced three sons and one daughter, but they would live to see the death of two of their sons. After their second son, Donald, died on April 2, 1940, Howard attended a revival at the Mountain Mission Church in Charleston, West Virginia. He listened to the preacher, Hobson Fisher, quote 2 Samuel 12:23, "But now he is dead, wherefore should I fast? Can I bring him back again? I shall go to him, but he shall not return to me."

Howard repeated that quotation countless times during the following years as he told the story of how he was saved just twenty days after his seven-year-old son had died of pneumonia. Each time he told the story, he said that spring of 1940 was the most beautiful he had seen in his life.

In August 1946, Howard was ordained a minister and became a member of the West Virginia Gospel Tabernacle Association. He would spend the remainder of his life as both a carpenter and a preacher, but always as a husband and father providing for his family.

Every holiday was special in the Withrow house. I know because I married the oldest son, Bill.

At Christmastime, Howard made candy, a skill he had learned during the Depression when he worked in a candy store on Quarrier Street in Charleston. I can still see the large marble slab on which he poured red sticky liquid that would harden into hot cinnamon candy. We family members gathered around the kitchen table and watched his hands as they deftly shaped the hardening substance into small candy canes.

If there was ever a Norman Rockwell scene, it was inside the

Withrow home. Whether it was Father's Day, the Fourth of July, or Christmas, the sons, the daughter, their spouses, and their offspring gathered at Howard and Ora's. After the death, though, of the youngest son, Paul, we could see the effects on both parents. They were growing tired, and their hearts had been broken twice.

Howard had told his daughter, Dolores, that he couldn't stand it if something ever happened to Ora.

He said, "I would want to die with her."

On March 14, 1989, just three months before their sixtieth wedding anniversary, Howard succumbed to leukemia. Ora stood at his bedside in St. Francis Hospital and said, "Howard, I'll meet you on the other side."

She kept her promise, going to meet him in September 1996.

Dolores said of her father, "Looking back, I know he showed his love by providing a living for all of us, and he worked hard. There was little time for anything else."

After Howard's death and after my mother-in-law, who had grown frail, had moved into her daughter's home, my husband and I went back to the empty home place.

I descended the wooden stairs my father-in-law had built. A few minutes later, I entered the small room where his screwdrivers, saws, and hammers still hung in a neat row on the walls behind his worktable, just as he had left them. I don't believe in ghosts, but as I stood in that empty room I could almost feel Howard's spirit in the room with me. I was suddenly filled with an awareness—an epiphany really—that even endings can be peaceful.

Through the years my father-in-law had been committed to his calling as a preacher, to his trade as a carpenter, and to his family as a husband and father.

The death of this remarkable couple marked the end of a chapter in our family and perhaps the end of an era as well.

II. REFLECTIONS

Your Turn

You may need to give up your day job, television, recreation, and maybe even meals—that is, if you've recently bought a mattress. Your new possession will soon possess you and your time. Every other week for the first three months, you must rotate that baby, placing the foot at the head and the head at the foot, according to the manufacturer's recommendations. Don't flip yet; just regularly rotate that 16-inch thick, heavy object. Rotating, therefore, will require at least two persons, preferably two stout persons. You can see that someone else's time will be consumed as well.

On each side of your mattress, you'll discover two handles. Don't be fooled. They're just decorative, not in any way functional. The manufacturer tells you in no uncertain terms that you're not to touch those handles. If you do and one pulls loose, your mattress will no longer be under warranty. Since the price is as hefty as the product, you obey.

As the mattress is rotated, onlookers stand nearby (folks enjoy watching these kinds of activities). The observers hear the rotators utter through gritted teeth words like bulky, cumbersome, awkward, and other unprintable expressions. This, of course, is the easy part of caring for this new thing that seems to have taken on a life of its own.

During alternate weeks, rotators become flippers. Now you can flip. The mattress must be flipped from right side up to right side down. Remember not to touch those handles.

Then another problem arises. How does one climb onto bedding, the top of which has expanded almost to the ceiling, and once there, how does one get out? I'm just a little over five feet tall. The salesman said I should buy a step stool, but I was determined to find my own way. I've learned that if I start running from the bedroom door, I can take a giant leap and, most of the time, make it. In the mornings, I'm wide awake by the time I hit the floor. It's little wonder folks sleep better on a new mattress.

Many manufacturers of other products also offer weird instructions and warnings. Our daughter has an iron with a warning not to iron clothes while wearing them, lest the buyer burn the body. A warning tag on at least one brand of stroller cautions the consumer not to fold the stroller while the baby is still in it. A tube of glue in my husband's shop has a warning that the glue should not be put into eyes. Labels on our mower caution workers to keep their feet and hands away from rotating blades. A label on sleeping pills cautions they may make one sleepy.

Our ladder lurks in the corner of the garage, waiting to cause an accident. It is labeled with so many warnings that the manufacturer had to reduce the print to include all the information. We should face the ladder when climbing it. We should not use it at all if we're in poor health. We shouldn't overreach. We can't climb on the back section or stand on the top shelf or the pail shelf (shucks). We shouldn't place it on a slippery surface, and we must be sure to open the ladder before climbing it. Also, we should keep both hands on the ladder. This means we can't use it while painting the house or cleaning the gutters.

Then, there are those products that must be put together. The parts, sometimes labeled A, B, and C, are measured by the metric system—a system that has about as much chance of catching on in this country as kilt-wearing opossum hunters. The moral of this story is if you see on the container of a product "some assembly required," run away fast; otherwise, you must deal not only with metric measurements, but also with a search to find instructions in English. Often, as many as three or four pages will contain at least as many languages, and the author probably doesn't speak English. This means the directions will make as much sense as if they had been written in Sanskrit.

Then there are the user-friendly computers. They used to come packed with a stack of books about a foot tall. Now the tutorial is hidden somewhere inside each computer's electronic guts. Bet you can't find it. You're about as well off to buy a new mattress. At least, you know what's expected. If you do, it's your turn to turn.

Revealing Clothes

You can tell a book writer by her cover—that is, by her attire. At a recent world-renowned writing conference, I made the observation that women writers have their own dress code, although they might be the last to admit to such vain thinking. Nonetheless, I discovered that the more serious, and therefore the more obscure a writer is, the more she dresses like, well, a bag lady. The usual costume is underscored with sandals of dull brown or black. Now, these sandals are clunky and, to my untrained eyes, ugly, but so much the better for the serious author who doesn't give a whit for appearances. It costs a great deal to be the carbon copy of a bag lady. The sandals alone must cost a fortune, for they are usually handmade of genuine leather or suede.

The drop-dead serious author, the one steeped in scholarly pursuits, combines this footwear with white socks. One writer attending the conference, though, wore heavy gray socks, the kind men in Antarctica would find suitable. The temperature at our festival was 105 degrees, and extreme heat warnings were announced periodically. The true literary writer wears a long printed skirt, fashionably wrinkled and unevenly hemmed. Instead of a tailored blouse, she wears a white undershirt, which sometimes is covered with a handcrafted vest. The no-nonsense female scribe never wears makeup, although she wears expensive lotions made of something totally natural like sea algae into which a few drops of genuine vanilla extract have been carefully blended. As an author passed me one day on the way to her poetry workshop, her eyes straight ahead on the target, I thought I could smell a yellow cake baking, but, no, it was the serious author cooking in the noonday sun. The hair of the grave writer is never coifed. Rather, hanging limp and straight, it is pulled back behind one or both ears. It is important to expose the earlobes, at least one, for this is where she can demonstrate her absolute commitment to multiculturalism. Her earrings may be made by Native Americans or perhaps by someone in Senegal. In any event, they speak of a culture other than the writer's own, and they dangle, always dangle.

Every profession has its dress code. The accountant, the banker, the lawyer can all be as serious with respect to clothing as the scholarly writer. They and their fellow business executives dress in cookie-cutter dark suits and power-color ties (at one time the 'in" color was red; at another, it was yellow). White long-sleeved shirts are the norm, although the donning of a pale pink shirt still shows real courage. If the executive is high enough in the pecking order, he can even wear a funky tie with words symbolizing one of his other identities. "Grandfather" or "Golfer" comes to mind.

The female executive, like her male counterpart, usually wears a business suit. She, however, never wears pink or ruffles or dangling earrings. Her skirts, for a time, were as short and revealing as those worn by ladies of the night, another kind of lady altogether. The heels of her shoes are no more than two and one-half inches tall, and like those of the serious author, her shoes are usually dull brown or black, although navy is acceptable. The spike heels that tilted women forward to a 90-degree angle have long since given way to chunky heels, each of which weighs almost as much as the weights the businesswoman lifts to stay fit.

Friday, of course, is the casual-dress day in the workplace, a day when both male and female can toss out the business apparel in favor of more comfortable attire. No jeans are allowed, however, even on TGIF. The fellows can replace their tasseled loafers with walking shoes, and the women can wear dress slacks, some of which are even made of polyester.

Teenagers have always had their own clothing preferences. Occasional remnants from the grunge period are blue jeans with the crotch hanging down to the knees. It is the back view of the guy wearing these jeans that turns heads, though, while at the same time turning the noun "moon" into a verb.

In preparation for the long-anticipated writing festival, I visited a trendy department store and asked the clerk for an outfit that would make me look like a bag lady. I explained that I would be among serious writers and I wanted to fit in. She got in the spirit of things right away. We found just the right long skirt and top. Then, she said, "Honey, go to the shoe department and get some water buffaloes."

I did, but the woman in the shoe department had never heard of water buffaloes, so I was left to my own devices. This means that for one fleeting evening at the farewell banquet where I wore my long skirt and suitable top, from the ankles up, I was pale-green cucumber cool. You would have known right away that I was a book writer, a serious writer, too. You would have known by my cover.

A Bush in the Hand

I have a secret, but soon you'll know my secret, too. August 1, 2000, ushered in by bright sunlight, was the day of George W. Bush's visit to West Virginia's Capitol grounds. I knew Bush's visit would provide me with an opportunity to see and photograph a future president (or at least a presidential candidate). What a story this would be for my descendants.

As I parked my car in one of the few spaces left (many blocks from the Capitol), I noticed that a blue-gray mist had settled over Charleston. Carrying my umbrella and camera, I began my long trek to the Capitol. After arriving at the War Memorial, I had to stand behind a long line of people who also realized the significance of the day. A state trooper told all of us to park our umbrellas under a tree (this wasn't going to be as much fun as I thought); only then could we join the crowd of approximately 5,000. Most were Bush supporters—including a few Democrats—although a small gathering of Gore backers remained at the edge of the crowd. They were well behaved and gracious.

I worked my way through the large crowd. Shorter than everyone in the audience except the children, I found it easy to finagle my way through clusters of onlookers until I was suddenly stopped by, of all things, a reddish-orange sawhorse. Much to my dismay, sawhorses surrounded a block of folding metal chairs. Most were occupied, although I saw four of five empty seats. I wondered why some folks deserved seats and some didn't. After about twenty minutes, a gray-haired lady (at least eighty) maneuvered her way in front of me. Seeing a guard behind the blockade, I asked him if he thought young men should be sitting when the lady in front of me had to stand. He agreed that was not good, so he pulled the sawhorse back to let her and her companion (her daughter?) through. Here's my secret. I quickly followed and was soon sitting beside a woman senator wearing a pale green jacket dress with her metal name tag partially under a lapel. The guard replaced the sawhorse, and there I was. The Marshall University Pep Band and others entertained us as we waited for almost an hour.

Soon, raindrops began falling, sparse at first, but the drops were soon large and plentiful. Talk about a bad-hair day. The good senator beside me pulled out her umbrella (mine was still under a tree somewhere) and a waterfall from her umbrella started to pour onto the center of my head; my glasses were glazed with water. I reached up and tipped her umbrella to the other side where the waterfall began to wet the head of the delegate on her other side. When the senator felt the tug on her umbrella, she turned and apologized.

I said, "Dear, if you could just move that bumbershoot this way a tad, my right side would stay drier." She did; it helped a little.

Finally, Governor Bush and Laura, his wife, arrived. I wouldn't have known that except for the applause from the crowd and the waving of tiny American flags and Bush-Cheny signs and the beating thwack of the red clappers. People stood and I was unable to see him.

Oh, yes, my camera. I have four snapshots of the back of a woman's straw hat and the back of a man's head. Each time I clicked the shutter, the couple in front of me moved their heads together. When I first poised my camera, I could see Governor Bush in the far distance, so I readied the zoom and captured each magnified straw of the woman's hat that blocked my view.

I had all the cheering aids—posters, flags, everything—because I was sitting with the VIPs. The reserved chairs reminded me of cultural events in the governor's mansion when a former governor, a Democrat, was at the helm. There was always a choice block of seats for the elite who could arrive late and who knew the velvet rope would guard their special chairs.

On that rainy day, as I sat in the downpour waiting for Governor Bush, I vowed that if ever I had the chance I would tell elected officials, both Democrats and Republicans, that they work for those of us who elect them. It's not the other way around. The public—especially aging veterans—should sit while public office holders stand in gratitude for the privilege of serving their state or nation.

A Cardinal Commitment

It was clear from the outset that he was a gentleman of the highest order—a rare bird. I watched quietly as he escorted her home. After she was safely inside, he lingered nearby for a few minutes to be sure all was well. Then, he left. He was soon back, though, hanging around like a love-struck teenager. Of course, I guess he was in love, for he would remain faithful to her above all others for the remainder of his life, and she would reciprocate. Fully devoted to each other, the two would be parted one day only by death itself.

Sitting alone on our front porch during one lime-green evening in mid-spring, I discovered a chance to observe something most people never get to see. An ornithologist would have been envious. From my catbird's seat, I felt like a voyeur, but I continued to watch nonetheless. Each day, after that special spring evening, I enjoyed from my secret place watching a love story unfold.

On that first day, I noticed a male cardinal walking in our front yard. Dressed in his brilliant red suit and matching top hat, he sported a black beard and mustache around his conical beak. He had found food that he carried carefully in his bill. He approached his nearby mate, and the two made contact, beak to beak. He placed the food he had gathered into her mouth. The pair then searched together for more food and soon visited the feeders in back of the house where they found an abundance of sun-flower seeds, their favorite.

Usually cardinals build their nests in thickets, briar tangles, and thick shrubbery or along the margins of woods and streams. Their nests are built no more than three or four feet from the ground. At the corner of our porch, a thick shrub must have looked like a good construction site because I noticed the couple began bringing in items for the exterior of their new home. I couldn't believe they would build so close to our house, but there it was. They wove on the outside sturdy materials, such as twigs, rootlets, and bits of bark. The interior, however, would be soft. The couple collected the most tender grasses, which would serve as a gentle lining for their new family. When completed, the nest would have made an engineer proud. It would withstand wind and rain and hail.

There are now two tiny red birds and one unhatched egg in the nest. The male still "walks" his mate to the door, then perches on a nearby limb of an apple tree where he keeps a wary watch over his family. Just after dawn, when daylight gray grows into a golden morning, he comes calling, giving his persistent chirp. She awakens, and the two go out to eat and gather food for their babies. They return together each time. Their days are spent nurturing their young. How different the cardinal is from the cowbird that lets the mother of another species raise her young. How different the cardinal is from other finches that fight one another for food as ferociously as the repugnant hummers. How loyal and gentle and caring the cardinal is. Little wonder that Audubon himself said of the northern cardinal, "in richness of plumage, elegance of motion, and strength of song, [the cardinal] surpasses all its kindred in the United States." People in Illinois, Indiana, Kentucky, North Carolina, Ohio, Virginia, and West Virginia must agree because each of these states has adopted the cardinal as its state bird.

Hearing that echoing chirp, chirp, chirp, I look again toward the shrub at the corner of our porch. There he is—that loyal and loving gentleman in red—waiting for his mate to awaken and go to breakfast with him. I wonder if he knows how important he is in seven states and beyond. I wonder if he knows he symbolizes much that is good in the world.

Accidental English

We know about doublespeak. We use it when we're trying to hide what we're actually saying or when we want to boost someone's self-esteem (a hyphenated darling of an expression). For example, when Mr. Grocery Store Owner wants to make a checkout clerk feel good about herself, he just changes her title to career associate scanning professional. We can even make street persons and criminals feel good with doublespeak. A street person is a nongoal-oriented member of society. A bank robber is simply an unauthorized person making an unauthorized withdrawal. We don't dare call someone a failure today; he or she is simply a fiscal underachiever. See how easy it is to charm folks into the surreal world of enhanced self-esteem. Of course, there's nothing accidental about doublespeak; it's a deliberate choice of words in an attempt to deceive. Language usage, though, is rife with pitfalls, and all of us occasionally fall into the linguistic pit.

If you think doublespeak bends the language, let me tell you about puzzlespeak or accidental English. My introduction to this form of language twisting came about when I taught English skills to college students. At the beginning of each semester, I gave an ungraded quiz. It had a twofold purpose: I wanted to get samples of my students' writing, and I wanted to discover what they knew about our culture, history, language, and the like.

Here are a few samples of their definitions and identifications.

When asked to define the term pro-life, one student wrote, "Pro-life means life after death."

Another student, defining apathy, wrote, "Apathy is a term used in the medical field to describe a person who is willing to die." Are you an apathy?

Paradox had a number of definitions, but here are a couple of the best ones: "two doctors" or "two docks side by side at the edge of a lake." Take your pick.

If you think Don Quixote is a character in a novel by Cervantes, think again. "Don Quixote is a South American drug lord," wrote one student.

Another said, "Don Quixote helps Juan Valdez pick coffee. He's one doggone good coffee picker."

"Circumlocution is when a dog goes 'round and 'round before taking a nap. He's circumlocuting."

"Oboe is a female hobo," or "a person's place of residence," or "a word used in poetry."

"*War and Peace* is a book written by Stephen King to try to show his funny side."

"Myopia is my own opinion about anything."

"Cain and Abel means one can walk well with a cain."

"A cappella - I hope this is a typo." Another wrote, "A cappella is part cap and part umbrella."

When asked to identify Betsy Ross, one student wrote a cheer:

"Betsy Ross, Betsy Ross, Betsy Ross bread/Look at the scoreboard and see who's ahead."

As you can see, I did get excellent examples of the students' prose, as well as an indication of what they knew, but mostly what they didn't know.

Accidental English, known as bloopers, often occurs in speech. One time, I was teaching the definition of the word epiphany. I meant to say, "Students, when you find epiphany in a novel or short story, you'll also probably find a shudder and a shiver."

That is not at all what I said. I transposed shudder and shiver, saying, "a shover and a shi. . . ." I dismissed the class, for the laughter overpowered my remaining comments, which were humble, to be sure. Every single student, though, wrote the correct definition of the word on the final exam. Eureka!

Word twins (homonyms) cause language accidents, too, especially in writing. Compliment and complement come to mind. When I entered a restaurant a few years ago, a sign over the salad bar offered this hand-written message: "Our fresh lettuce compliments our hamburgers." I could just see the lettuce saying, "Boy, you're one good-looking hamburger." Of course, the writer should have used complement, meaning to complete or to enhance.

Then one evening, I heard an internationally known television announcer say, "I've been on that diet, and it just made me nauseous." She meant nauseated, because nauseous refers to whatever makes us nauseated. Those twin words cause lots of accidents.

Whether it's doublespeak, puzzlespeak, or other kinds of tormented English, the language is all we have to communicate our ideas and feelings. Watch the pitfalls.

All-American Pastime

Early morning mist shrouds the trees surrounding our home, but soon late August sun burns through to reveal the perfect day for a yard sale. Laden with everything from old dishes to knife sharpeners to collectibles and, er, antiques, our tables are placed at strategic outdoor sites to catch the attention of potential buyers. Strung from tree to tree and porch post to porch post, ropes droop with heavy loads of merchandise. Like the soft side of Sears, our store has clothing, soft to the touch and lovely to behold. Ours is easy on the pocketbook because it's been ever so gently used.

Build it and they will come. They do.

The first to arrive at most garage or yard sales are savvy and not-so-savvy antique dealers. At least an hour before the action begins, their vans are lined up on the driveway. Each dealer sits patiently behind the steering wheel, watching while items are being brought out and arranged for display. Sharp-eyed, they squint through dusty windshields to see if anything worthy of resale is available. As if on cue, these retailers get out of their vans almost simultaneously, for one can't get ahead of the other. Moving as deftly as ballet dancers between tables of porcelain, they pick up each piece, searching the bottom for marks that might indicate factory and date. They bypass the clothing, eyeing only those objects that speak of yesteryear or scream of fad-resale possibility. The knowledgeable dealers can quickly distinguish between a collectible and an antique. They conduct their tour within minutes, buy only the valuables, and leave quickly.

Next in line, is the potential buyer who is a devoted *Antiques Road Show* viewer. This buyer is looking for that quarter vase that's really worth at least $50,000. In my yard, one such viewer holds a small vase she's lifted from a table. With dreamy eyes, she looks far into the distance and gently turns the vase over and over in her hands. I know what she's doing. She's fantasizing about seeing herself on the *Antiques Road Show*. She sees herself finally at the head of the line where she stands at the table.

There, the expert looks at her vase and says, "What can you tell me about the background of your vase?"

She smiles demurely and says, "I bought it for a quarter at Dolly's yard sale."

The antique expert then asks, "Do you have any idea of the value of this piece?"

Smiling coyly, she says, "No, I don't."

He says, "Would you be surprised if I told you it's worth $125,000?"

She says softly, "Wow!"

Coming out of her reverie, she hands me a quarter for the small pink vase and saunters back to her car. I feel uneasy. Maybe I should have priced that vase at fifty cents.

Most men who frequent yard sales are looking for tools; men like them. Then, there's the handy man. He looks for old things that can be repaired and used or resold. One man at my sale looks at an old propane gas grill.

I'm planning to offer him money to haul it off when he says, "I'll give you $10 for your grill. I fix 'em and resell 'em."

"Well," says I, "I was thinking more of $15, but I'll let it go for $10. You look like a nice person." Such is the yard-sale game.

The next type to take part in this favorite American pastime is the compulsive shopper. Whether the shopping takes place in a fine department store, a novelty roadside stand, or a front yard makes no difference to this consumer. This shopper comes ready to purchase something. One such customer looks at a table filled with trinkets. She buys several pairs of beads without clasps, so they can't be worn. She buys candles bent from heat, so they can't be burned. She doesn't care. She never quibbles about price; she just buys. I like her.

A typical yard sale frequenter is the browser. This person is not at all interested in spending money. She just wants to see what is on display. Maybe she's writing a book about the wares offered at yard sales. She whips around the tables, flips through the clothes, looks askance at the broken sweeper, and runs to her car. Another browser has passed through like a chilly breeze.

Most customers, by far, are bargain hunters. They are not to be confused with those looking for that rare and priceless object. This yard sale consumer just wants a good bargain, which is different from a "steal." Low prices and lots of merchandise, then, provide the key to a successful yard sale. I mean really low prices. Bargain hunters will haggle over a few cents. "Are you sure you won't take less than fifty cents for this?" asks one woman, with a frown as sour as an upside down lemon slice. She's pointing to a blouse with the sales tag still hanging from its sleeve. It reads $25.

Pine trees in back of our house rise to meet a scarlet sunset. It's been a long day, so I say, "Sure, you can have that new blouse for a quarter."

She pays me and heads toward her new car.

I count my day's loot and divide my hours into the amount. Within the past three days, I've made fifty cents an hour. Still, I've had fun and have cleaned out the junk and gems from my house. Now, to watch that woman on the *Antiques Road Show*, the one who bought my pink vase.

Cars Recalled

"Fords recalled." That was the lead into a make-believe television program on an old Bob Newhart sit-com. George, the host of the show within a show, wanted to lure more viewers to his program. He came up with the advertising blurb "Fords recalled." It worked. Folks gathered around their television sets in record numbers, watching to see if their cars were being recalled. What they saw was a lineup of guests discussing their recollections of their first Fords.

Facing increasing competition, television executives are trying the same tack in an effort to attract more viewers. Only the warnings are not supposed to be make-believe. The hype of Y2K is a typical example. The predictions of computer glitches and terrorist bombings were not supposed to be make-believe, but you never know. Of course, the economy received a good boost. We shoppers stood in long lines behind carts piled high with bottled water, batteries, bread, and other provisions. In retrospect, it was a silly thing to do, but we just couldn't help ourselves. We reasoned it was better to be prepared, just in case the experts knew what they were doing. Silly, silly us (I couldn't bring myself to write, "silly we").

Like George's car recall, though, the continual warnings work. We are lured into watching the news every day, lest we miss a warning and perish due to lack of knowledge. If Y2K predictions weren't enough to scare us out of our proverbial wits, then weather forecasts might do the job—that is, when we can understand them.

Even the titles of local weather teams have a threatening ring to them: Storm Team, Storm Tracker, and First Warning. A past governor may be the forerunner of such ominous weather predictions. Former Governor Jay Rockefeller issued dire warnings of an oncoming blizzard. He told us to stay inside and take care of our senior citizens. We were scared. Trying to beat others to grocery stores where every last loaf of bread would disappear from shelves, drivers zoomed up and down highways, their tires screeching and horns blowing. Waiting for the blizzard, I remember looking out the window. The sun had come out, and it stayed and stayed for the whole day and the next. The blizzard never materialized. I was told it was more than a year before Rockefeller could even smile about the event. We must remember, though, that he received his information from meteorologists. I don't know whether they had Doppler to help them then or not.

Technology has moved with a vengeance onto the weather forecasting scene. After a couple of TV anchors and the sports commentator chat with one another about the weather—ignoring us viewers completely—they finally turn to the expert. He or she stands in front of a map of the United States. We can see fronts move across the map. Clouds roll over states so minuscule we're not always sure which states are cloud-covered, but the clouds continue to move across the country. Snow and rain and sun all do their thing, right there on the TV screen. We watch. The Alberta clips her way down from Canada, bringing frigid air over the northern and western states. We patiently watch and wait. We are told of cold fronts and warm fronts. Vertical air masses and slanting air masses are all over the place. A low-pressure system's here, and a high-pressure system's there. The wind is steady at 14 mph, and the barometer is 29.7, and the old Doppler shows another cold front coming our way. Whoa! I tell you it's more than we ever want to know. We just want to know whether the weather is going to cause us to carry an umbrella, shovel snow, or wear sunglasses. That and the temperature will do it for most of us. The weather has become news, even when it's not.

Our evening news is beset with warnings of food contamination, hospital mistakes, bomb threats, and the list goes on. Oh, yes, you'll want to watch to see if your car is being recalled.

Chapter Endings

Closing down the third and last section of our popular restaurant in mid-September, I experience an empty feeling. I have no choice, though, for all our pugnacious, independent diners, because of fewer daylight hours, have already left to travel south where they will continue to enjoy warm sunshine and colorful flowers. Every fall, they leave us poor folks to face the onslaught of winter and the continual weather warnings on television, warnings preceded by chiming bells or harsh buzzes. Each winter, with the first few flakes of snow predicted, these ominous reports, disguised as news, silently march across the bottom of our television screens. We're told yet again how to dress warmly, how to drive in snow, and how to avoid over-exertion from shoveling the "white stuff," most TV announcers' favorite substitution for the word snow. Long gone, our smart summer diners miss all that. I'll bet that's the real reason they leave.

To be sure, our summer clientele are shrewd. They never pay for their meals; they don't even sing for their supper. Rather, they entertain us with food fights that make college cafeteria chaos look tame. Our customers, when they're not bellying up to the bar, wildly dive-bomb one another and sometimes sit for hours just protecting food they no longer want. Mad as hatters, they zoom around their seats and frighten other diners far away from the restaurant. Known to chase away diners a hundred times their size, these raging dynamos, each no larger than the little finger, return to stand guard over unwanted food once more.

During the sweltering months of July and August, these voracious eaters keep me busy. Each day, I prepare their favorite food, which they slurp through built-in straws. I carefully measure two cups of sugar with eight cups of water. I boil the mixture about two minutes and let it cool. Then I clean their dining places, making sure no mildew remains in their eating utensils.

Studies have indicated that humming birds are healthiest when their feeders are kept clean and they are fed exactly one part sugar to four parts water (no artificial sweeteners). The tiny creatures are worth the trouble. The ruby-throated hummers, so named because of the bright red throat of the male, are the smallest of all birds, and they frequent our West Virginia hills. With wings beating at about 75 times per second, these tiny birds can move forward at 60 miles per hour. What is more, they travel thousands of miles each spring and return to the same bird feeder. Amazing! I know people who get lost just walking around a small shopping mall. Even drivers armed with maps, compasses, and those contraptions that say, "turn left at the next corner," get lost, oh, so lost. No one knows how the humming bird finds its way back to the same yard and the same feeder year after year, but those bird watchers who put small bands on tiny bird legs have kept careful track of the comings and goings of hummers.

As I sat on our front porch recently, I looked at the empty spaces where only a few weeks before hanging feeders lured hummers, their wings moving so rapidly I could hear the familiar humming sound. I was reminded of endings in life and how they're like chapter endings in books. I recalled the last college class I taught in December 1994. One student remained, like the last hummer of the season. Smiling, she placed her final exam on my desk, wished me the best, and walked out the door. The room was suddenly empty and quiet. I sat there knowing I would not "come this way again." Beyond the windows lay yet another beginning, a new chapter.

I had taught my students that everything, especially each of their essays, must have a beginning, a middle, and an end. The truth is, though, life is cyclic. Endings lead to beginnings, and life's rhythm beats ever onward. Birth, life, death. Sunrise, noonday, sunset, night. Spring, summer, autumn, winter. The pulse of life, chaotic though it may seem, is as ordered and structured as a spider's web glistening in the autumn sun. As I look beyond the empty spaces where three bird feeders hung only a few weeks ago, I know the hummers will return, along with the renewal of spring. My empty feeling gives way to anticipation, to the cycles of life itself.

Cultural Cornucopia

The United States is experiencing a virtual cornucopia of cultures, so much so that the term "multiculturalism" has been bandied about almost as much as the word "relationship." Shucks, I guess I'm about as cultured as most Appalachians except I don't own a baseball cap that I can wear backwards at the dinner table. But being cultured and having a culture are not the same. The truth is I don't have a culture to call my own. I don't even know who my ancestors were back beyond my grandparents, and I never knew my paternal grandfather because in the early '20s four policemen fatally shot him as he waited to become the next governor of West Virginia. I was not born yet. My Aunt Phyllis assured me before her natural death, though, that my grandfather was to be on the Democratic ticket and would be elected the next governor of our politically oriented state. The machine had already declared it to be so. The front page of a yellowed Charleston Gazette newspaper has headlines announcing my grandfather's death, and under the headlines are details of his demise. My point is that the only tradition I embrace is having no tradition at all. In short, like most Appalachians, I'm a cultural orphan. I'm sure if I were to trace my ancestry back far enough I would find royalty somewhere. Isn't that why folks keep digging down into their ancestral roots? That's why I'd do it, but what I found just going back to Grandfather Wood was far from a blue-blood line, although he was purported to be a genius on days when he wasn't enjoying the fruits of his part-time labor—home-brew. When he was killed, he was postmaster general in Charleston and before that had been a steamboat captain, an artist, an engineer, and the first councilman of the First Ward in Charleston, West Virginia. Despite his weakness for "the drink," I think I would have liked him. When I look at his baby picture with his unblinking eyes staring straight at me, I feel a spiritual link to him. Still, I don't think that's enough to say I have a culture, that I'm part of a long tradition.

Wondering if mountain music might give me a culture, I thought about the dulcimer. Then, as quickly, I thought of my mother's experience with the hourglass shaped instrument. She'll be ninety in four months and has lived in Appalachia all her life. After attending a performance of

authentic mountain music, she phoned me. Two women had played dulcimers, and my mother said, "They played some kind of instrument I'd never
heard of. It started with 'dull.' Anyway, I didn't know one song they played,
so it was boring."

The dulcimer is believed to have made its first appearance in the
Appalachian Mountains sometime in the late 1800s. Some scholars believe
that, but not my mother because her mother before her had never men-
tioned the instrument either. I myself like the dulcimer (*dulcis* means sweet
and *melos* means song), but my Appalachian mother and grandmother give
me doubts as to its authenticity as an Appalachian invention. My own
encounter with this instrument was at a festival where a trio of out-of-state
yuppies, dressed like Appalachians of yesteryear, played dulcimers. I'm
not about to claim the dulcimer, then, as part of my heritage since musi-
cians from another place introduced me to it.

Perhaps language could provide a cultural thread for me. According to *The Oxford Companion to the English Language*, Appalachian English is not a kind of Elizabethan or Shakespearean English as many people
believe it to be. Rather, according to the *Companion to the English Language*, it is merely a dialect that uneducated folks who live in the mountains of southeastern United States speak. Well, now, that gives others and
me problems because we love nothing better than to discuss points of language usage, and we're all Appalachians. Language, then, won't give us a
continuous thread of tradition.

For now, we'll remain cultural orphans while the word
"multiculturalism" continues to veneer the land.

Diet Right

As my mother and I sat on the front porch of my country home, a backdrop of autumn foliage and the sun-washed landscape of late October provided a cheerful morning setting.

The whole scene had the makings of a good day when Mother suddenly squinted her left eye almost shut, looked at me, and said, "Dolly, you're just like Marie. She drinks diet colas all the time, and she's not overweight. I don't think either one of you is fat."

See. I said it was going to be a good day.

Then, she squinted that one eye tightly shut and added, "You both have bellies that stick out, though."

Everything on me sagged even more. I have to admit that when I approach the salad bar in a restaurant, my stomach arrives a few minutes before I do. Ah, if I only lived in the Golden Age of Greece, my shape would be in style. Big bellies on women were objects of beauty then. Some poet, like Keats, could have written an ode to a Grecian tum, but alas, in 1999, I'm living on the threshold of a new millennium, and big bellies are out there and out of style.

We nonetheless have our ideals even as the Greeks did. We've all heard you can't be too rich or too thin. Of course, that's just a maxim we keep on a pedestal, up high and out of reach, something to strive for in our dreams or in an expensive diet program. Even as we watch models, tall and gaunt, float across a stage—wearing clothes we wouldn't be caught dead in—we envy their svelte figures. Turning this way and that, the bony models, with shoulder blades sticking up like cricket legs, stroll slowly from one end of the platform to the other. Their slow gait is probably as much due to hunger as to the desire to display the designer clothing.

Our obsession with being thin is intensified by these models, as well as by Hollywood stars and television actors. They all are cut from the same slender cookie mold. In fact, just recently obesity in our country was called an epidemic, which I think means you can "catch" it, and many of us have caught it. The result of all this obsession is if we're not thin, we're suffering from either dieting or feeling guilty.

Those bright folks who focus more on getting rich than getting thin entice millions of Americans each year to enroll in some sort of diet program. One of my friends has joined one such program. She now eats a high-protein and low-carbohydrate diet, which consists of all the bacon, ham, eggs, and sausage she wants. She claims her cholesterol has gone down. Another friend is in a low-protein and high-carbohydrate diet, which means she can have all the bread, pasta, potatoes, and the like she wants.

The diet gurus are quick to tell you that you must exercise, along with following your calorie-deprived diet, if you want the best results. Since calories are energy units, your energy will not be as high. This, of course, is not what folks tell you who are in the midst of an exercise-diet program. They look better, feel better; they have more energy than ever. Ah-ha, but notice how long they stay in such a program. That tells the story.

If you want to get thin and avoid all that exercise and awful taste-less food (calories are the flavor buds, you know), then you can buy a magic pill and lose weight. You might die in the process, however. Right now, there's a great deal of fanfare over fen-phen, that wonder-ingredient that is still in one or two existing diets despite warnings it may do a great deal of damage to various body parts. If all else fails, you can get a tummy-tuck or liposuction and have all that blubber sucked right out of there. I think there's danger in that, too. Body sculpting might be good. There's a roadside stand not far from where I live that specializes in body sculpting. There's also a home remedy. Just tightly bandage the old tum-tum with plastic wrap and leave it in place for some time. Notice after removing the wrap how the inches have fallen away. After a few hours, those nasty inches return, but you look good for a while.

In addition to the many diet programs, there are self-help groups. They cost much less (nominal costs, actually), but there usually is no pro-fessional person to work one-on-one with each participant. If none of this appeals to you, then try a high fiber diet. There's even something new on the market that will make the calories slip right on out. Nothing much remains in you for nutritional purposes. We must, after all, do something about this epidemic.

I'm going to share my secret diet, but don't tell anyone. Someday, I may want to charge a lot of money for distributing it. For breakfast, I eat one-half slice of dry (and, therefore, tasteless) toast, a boiled egg, and a cup of black coffee. For lunch, I have fruit and cottage cheese (just two table-spoonfuls of the cheese). For dinner, I have baked fish or chicken, a naked baked potato, and asparagus without butter or margarine. For a bedtime snack, I eat a package of chocolate-chip cookies, two tall glasses of milk, and if I'm still hungry, anything else I want. It works for me. I'm not overweight; I just have a large belly.

Doorknob Salute

During the green days of my high school years, I was invited to join a social sorority. Naïve and eager to belong, I was ecstatic. For someone from Dog Town (a pejorative label for my part of town), I thought I had come a long way. I was about to join "high society." Despite my youth—I was seventeen—as early as the initiation itself, I began to have misgivings. Draping white sheets around us like saris, we carried burning candles of different colors and marched around a large room. We chanted platitudes about loyalty, service, and truth (the last of which would surely be deleted today). Like looking through a foggy glass, I vaguely remember kneeling at one point and having trouble arising because the blasted sheet kept pulling me back to the floor. As I knelt, my sheet had caught on the heels of my shoes. I stumbled and fumbled and finally got to my feet. I was beginning to feel as silly as a goose in a gown. Trying to get up, I simultaneously struggled to hold back laughter—the kind that bubbles up unbidden in a teenager. I stuck with the group for less than a year when graduation mercifully set me free. Today, I grin knowingly as I look at the yellowed newspaper photo in which my fellow sorority sisters and I—all smug and smiling—form an exclusive circle around a long mahogany table that boasts a silver tea set and porcelain dishes. The afternoon tea was held in a large house at the opposite end of the city where I lived.

After graduation from high school, I became a secretary and, once again, was invited to join an organization, this one for career women. I must look like a joiner. I accepted the invitation, and much to my surprise, the initiation was similar to the one I had experienced in high school.

Candles and rituals and abstractions still ruled the rites of passage. This time, I was a quitter. I gave it up.

Not all organizations require initiations. After marriage with children, I joined the Parent Teacher Association (PTA). I became a homeroom mother and spent time with other homeroom mothers discussing whether we should serve vanilla wafers or chocolate cookies at various events. One time in Louisiana, I even became a fortune-teller. I sat in a tent with a crystal ball and gave young students good predictions about their future. That was fun, and the money collected at the school carnival went for a good cause. If I were still a young mother, would I be a homeroom mother again? You bet I would.

The next organization I remember was Midget League. I didn't belong, but I attended every football game in which our tiny, underweight son played. Before each game, we recited the pledge to our flag, but there was a small problem. We couldn't find the flag. There was none, so we spectators stood under the hot autumn sun, facing in different directions, with hands over hearts, saluting nonetheless. An alien flying over in a spaceship would have wondered about us. Sitting on a bleacher, I listened to the usual weekly criticisms about the coaches not letting certain boys play, how the coaches' sons always got to play. The players themselves seemed happy, but parents were often angry.

When I was invited to join an academic sorority in college, I asked the professor if I had to wear a sheet. She assured me I didn't. As an older college student, I remember our French professor telling us that women in France did not join organizations, that they were surprised American women liked them so. I can't account for that either. Yet I know that every few years, I join another one.

In fact, as years passed, I eventually joined an association with worthwhile causes. At the beginning of each meeting, we also saluted the flag. This time, we were inside a large room. Again there was no flag, and I remember facing the doorknob, with hand over heart, solemnly saluting.

I once declined an invitation to be a joiner, though, and am probably still the target of some disdain. The members smile a lot, hug one another, and see only the good things in life. They are really wonderful people. I had just left the college campus, though, where I had taught for many years—a place where cynicism was a mark of distinction. The bridge from rank cynicism to pure optimism was one I was not yet conditioned to cross.

Today, as I write this, I've been invited to join another group, one so new it's still searching for a name. I'll keep you posted.

Dropping the Handkerchief

In a quaint Iowa restaurant one summer, I was enjoying the company of four other writers as we dined around a large table. An award-winning novelist sat beside me. When the discussion turned to eyeglasses (I can't remember why), we agreed that we should not clean them with tissues, but we couldn't come up with a ready alternative.

The novelist said, "I use my cotton underpants."

Smiling sheepishly, I asked, "When you're dining out with a male, aren't you afraid you might send the wrong message if you whip out a pair of cotton panties and begin wiping your glasses?"

She agreed that might not be a good idea. The question of what to use to clean glasses was left unanswered. Then, I thought of women's handkerchiefs. Whatever happened to them? Like many other useful things, they've disappeared from the American scene. My mother recently gave me about fifteen of these cloth relics that she had saved from the '40s. Two must have been Christmas gifts because they have red poinsettias embroidered on the corners. Some boast images of other flowers and various designs. Others, still surprisingly white, are edged with one-inch matching borders of lace. Each is a miniature work of art. Despite their beauty, they were functional in their day. A woman walking in the park could drop her handkerchief just to get a nearby male to retrieve it for her. The hankie was a flirting device and far more subtle than, well, underpants. Drop the handkerchief—a popular game before PlayStation and Power Rangers came on the scene—could not have been played without something to drop. Don't confuse drop the handkerchief with hanky-panky; that's another kind of game entirely. When attending funerals, women took their best handkerchiefs. Kerchiefs were also used in church services where ladies—often moved by the spirit—wept unashamedly, dabbing at their tears with you know what. Planned obsolescence resulted in many things we use briefly and toss out. The paper tissue, discarded after one use, replaced women's handkerchiefs. The problem is we can't use tissues for cleaning eyeglasses or flirting or playing games. With the disappearance of women's hankies, part of our culture disappeared, too.

Then, there's the notion we once had of the man in the moon. He's been replaced by the man on the moon. Since the lunar landing and subsequent scientific discoveries of moon rocks and craters, any romance connected with the moon has vanished. "It's Only a Paper Moon," "Blue Moon," and "Moon over Miami," are songs that have lost their romantic messages. In fact, they've virtually disappeared, too. The harvest moon doesn't shine "for me and my gal" anymore. Today, the moon is merely Earth's dark satellite, getting its only light from the sun. Even moonlight has lost its magic.

Relaxation, the kind that demands nothing more than sitting and staring into space, has disappeared. At one time, the mark of a thinker was his or her ability to sit in a quiet place for hours and meditate. Poets, artists, philosophers—all creative persons and geniuses—required solitude in order to recharge or to think through a problem. Today, the mark of a successful person is busyness. People are busy, busy, busy and proud of it. The busier people are, the better. If demanding careers leave any spare time (many don't), that time can be filled with organizations and soccer and little league and midget league and scouts and committees. Meals are nuked in the microwave to save more time for activities. Family members who once caught up on the day's events around the dinner table now eat separately. We must be forever active. There is no time for thinking, for good conversation, for human connection.

The best visits used to take place on large front porches, now no more than perches. Today, porches have been added as an afterthought if, indeed, they've been added at all. Those that pretend to be old-fashioned are not even deep enough to accommodate a swing or two rockers where an old couple, having long ago committed themselves to an enduring marriage, can rock contentedly in the evening of their lives.

Losses in the path of progress have signaled the loss of innocence itself, the loss of a nation's childhood. It's enough to make us weep, but we have nothing with which to wipe our tears and no time for weeping anyway. Somewhere along the way, we've dropped the handkerchief and, oh, so much more.

Entitled

Whether rich men, poor men, beggar men, thieves, doctors, lawyers, or Indian chiefs, most Americans love their titles. I'll rewrite that sentence, though, conforming to political correctness when possible. Whether privileged persons, economically challenged persons, sticky-fingered disordered persons, doctors, or Native American chiefs, most Americans love their titles. In fact, titles in our society are as cherished as mom, apple pie, and Beanie babies.

A few savvy speakers and rhetoricians use attorney when addressing lawyers, but very few. Rhetorician is the preferred title or label scholarly writers use when referring to themselves—that is, when they're not using scholar.

Titles—like height, gender, and eyeglasses—affect us in strange ways. I remember a professor who had just earned her doctoral degree. We faculty members were attending commencement exercises. Looking for all the world like penguins, we stood in small groups, wearing our black robes and mortarboards. As we waited to march down the aisle, I noticed my colleague was distressed. When I asked what was wrong, she pointed to the three black stripes on each sleeve of her black robe, black on black. I could see the problem, for the stripes were barely visible.

"Who," she asked in desperation, "will even know I've earned my Ph.D., Dolly?"

Having the greatest sympathy for her plight, I said, "I know. I'll get some glue, spread it over your stripes and sprinkle glitter on the glue. Then, during the commencement exercises, I'll aim at the stripes with a flashlight, snapping it off and on to signal your doctoral stripes. That way, everyone will see them."

She didn't think that was funny and strutted quickly into another small group of penguins.

At another commencement, a colleague refused to march at all because the robe that was ordered for her had no stripes, and she was, as we all knew, a doctor. She refused to march down the aisle without the telltale stripes, so important was her title to her.

One summer, I had lunch with a woman who raised her shoulders and chin to their limits, looked straight across the table at me, and explained how she had been shunned in her writing workshop. She had been asked to read last after everyone was weary of hearing others' writing. She added, "And I'm full professor, too." I knew she meant she was at the top of the faculty ladder, but I couldn't help but wonder if she meant she had eaten quite enough.

The medical profession has its own hierarchy to which I'm not privy, but I know it's there as surely as Emily Dickinson knew heaven was there without seeing the map. I do know about ophthalmologists, optometrists, and opticians. The longer the title, the more education the doctor has and the higher he or she is on the title pole.

At the beginning of each semester, students wondered how they should address me. One semester, I told them the story of Eleanor Roosevelt when she met a young sailor who addressed her as Eleanor. She was the First Lady of the United States; now there's a title for you. Quick-witted, she replied something like this: "Don't be so formal, son. Just call me Toots."

I told my students they could call me Professor Withrow or Dolly, as long as they did it with respect, but Toots was a bit informal. The rest of the semester, I was Toots. One day, walking across the campus with our college president (another title for you), I heard a student's voice from afar. He yelled and waved at me, "Hey, Toots, how are you?"

The president's eyebrows shot upward in surprise. As I waved to the student, I gave the president my best sheepish grin and said, "It's a long story." He shook his head from side to side, but I saw his own small grin before he escaped into his office.

Certified public accountants will tell you, if you're interested, that there's a difference between a CPA and a mere accountant. I think there's a difference, too, between an accountant and a mere bookkeeper. Titles set up a hierarchy, which is why they are so significant. They make us feel important; they make us feel as if we're really somebody—that is, until a higher-titled somebody enters our corner.

There are those rare folks who have a sense of self-worth regardless of titles. I read one time about a janitor (now called a custodian) who loved his job because he cleaned a large library and, therefore, had access to a world of books. He not only enjoyed the rich environment of his workplace, but also he felt secure in his job. He knew no one else would be clawing at the corporate ladder or at his back to take his position away from him. He was happy with what most of us would perceive to be a lowly job, accompanied by a lowly title. Oh, yes, he was also a genius, but we would have known that without the article's giving his high IQ.

I know a true scholar, a doctor, who teaches at an Ivy League institution. He has asked me to call him by his first name, although I've never met him in person. We've written to each other about writing and books and ideas. We've also talked by phone.

He said one time, "Dolly, don't call me professor, scholar, or doctor. Call me Curt."

Do I think he is rare, special? You bet I do. Despite his accomplishments, despite his having written wonderful books, despite his being a world-class translator of Yiddish into English, he remains humble. So whether you're a doctor or an economically challenged person, whether you're an American Indian or, like most of us, mixed without a culture, you are important, all titles aside.

First Day of School

They feign a dread of the first day of school, those students who are returning, those who have been there before. Secretly, they are eager to get started once more, but it wouldn't be prudent to let others know of their excitement. Summer has grown tired, ragged around the edges. Roses and geraniums have faded, and the sun has taken on that mellow golden glow, producing "a certain slant of light," a phrase Emily Dickinson has made famous in one of her poems.

With each passing day now, we get about a minute less of daylight, which satisfies students because all the games have been played over and over again anyway. The swimming pool has lost its appeal, and talk among young children and adolescents has dwindled to a few words, except for the trite word " bored."

By summer's end, it looms large, that word, and mothers have grown tired of hearing it and of hearing the question, "What can I do now? I'm bored." Mothers have run out of ideas, and secretly (it wouldn't be wise for them to let others know either), they are also looking forward to that day when their homes are for a time quiet and empty. Ah, the silence, the sweetness of it all.

Here's an example of how mothers really feel. Our daughter said to Bonnie Thomas, another mother, "Summer's almost over. It's time again for school to start. It's rather sad, isn't it?"

Bonnie, not one to hide her feelings, said "Oh, come on now. You'll be doing cartwheels in the front yard on that first day." Blushing, they both laughed as the revealing floodlight of truth stood between them.

Kim, another friend of our daughter, gets together with several other mothers on the morning of that most wonderful day. They go out to break-fast at a nearby restaurant, hungry—not so much for food—but for adult conversation, for a common turf on which to expound their own concerns and views. During the brief breakfast, they are individuals, catering only to their own needs.

Unlike the experienced student, children who are going to school for the very first time let the world know of their combined fear and enthu-siasm. In their tender young worlds, they know not of pretense, of hidden feelings. Their mothers, too, openly display anxieties about sending their babies into an indifferent world.

Entering a school building for the very first time is for these tiny children like the first time one sees the ocean or sees snow or rides in a plane. There is something about firsts that stick with us for a lifetime. It is on that initial day that these youngsters begin to realize they are not the center of the universe. What a revelation that is. They start to understand that their requests may not be granted or even heard. All at once, they are one of many, no longer just one to be loved and pampered. Their com-ments, their opinions, their raised hands are sometimes ignored, for the teacher cannot cater to the special demands or even the fears of each stu-dent. Suddenly, the child's world has expanded beyond the protective walls of home. It is a jarring reality, and the only comfort to both child and parents is that we've all survived the beginning of school.

Most important, though, is what students do throughout the school year. Somehow, everyone—students, parents, and teachers—survive that first hectic day. For students, it is the day-to-day routine of both fall and spring semesters that can get as jagged, as weary and, yes, as boring as late summer itself.

One time, when I was an after-dinner speaker where high school graduates were being honored for their academic achievements, I stressed that their successes throughout their school years, beginning with that first day, were their successes and not anyone else's. Even with the help of dedicated teachers and loving parents, young people can fail if they choose to fail. Conversely, with the worst home environment, they can choose to succeed if they want success badly enough. We've all seen students emerge victorious from the worst circumstances. In today's society, we too often blame someone else when students fail or misbehave or even commit crimes. We find excuses for every negative behavior. We blame parents, educators, even society. I told those students that they alone had to continue making decisions that would create the quality of life they wanted.

For all you students who are going back to school, then, remember that attitude IS everything. If you want to feign dreading that first day, go ahead. Deep in the secret pocket of your heart, though, remain enthusiastic about school, no matter what, because enthusiasm breeds success.

Frankly Speaking

It all began innocently enough. The call came on an icy morning in late winter. The caller asked if I would be willing to serve on a panel discussion for her group of professional secretaries. She said I would discuss my good organizational skills. When I said I had none, she insisted I had to be an organized person because I had attended college late in life while, at the same time, caring for a family. This woman was a stranger, but she knew a great deal about me. I decided it would be fun, that there would be nothing for me to do but eat a delicious lunch and look important while sitting at the panel's table. I could just agree with the other panel members, nodding occasionally, so I accepted her invitation. Later, feeling guilty, I wrote a letter to her in which I again tried to convince her that I was anything but organized. It didn't work.

About a month later, I entered Cagney's restaurant ready to have a good time. I soon discovered there were three other members on the panel. As I talked with them during the luncheon, I discovered something else. There was no panel. Each was prepared to make a brief speech. There I sat with nothing to say. Fortunately, I had with me a copy of the letter I had written to the caller. I would read it. As the woman—tall, svelte, and self-assured—introduced me, she told her fellow members she hoped I would one day write a humorous book, that my letter to her was hilarious. She proceeded to read it. Her listeners were appreciative. I was—dare I say it?—speechless. In thirty seconds, I would be in front of that mike, dumbstruck. I thought about fainting, but I'm no wimp. I decided to tell those professional secretaries how to get registered and enroll in college classes. I didn't receive a standing ovation (darn!). That wasn't the worst experience I've had though.

I was to speak in Fayetteville, West Virginia. The auditorium at the high school was filled with folks waiting to hear me present a one-day workshop. The night before the session, my husband and I stayed at a nearby motel where neighbors partied until early morning. I didn't sleep. The next day, as I was being introduced, I leaned on the maroon velvet curtain, the kind that most school auditoriums have. Of course, it didn't hold my weight, so I fell to the floor of the stage. The audience (they knew me from the previous year's workshop) burst into uncontrollable laughter. The person introducing me had to stop because she couldn't control her laughter either. Unharmed, I got up as gracefully as I could under the circumstances, walked to the front of the stage and told the audience to remember when they evaluated me at day's end that I had fallen for them. At the conclusion of the session, I learned my audience thought I had fallen on purpose—just to break the ice—their words.

Most folks fear public speaking only second to death itself, and I can tell you that pretending the members of the audience are naked doesn't help. I remember the first time I was to give a workshop several years ago. As stressed as most people would be, I began my preparation by getting, not just one fever blister, but a whole cluster. Then, I got bronchitis a week before I was to speak to a group of CPAs (they are no-nonsense folks). I thought I would have to whisper, but I was determined not to cancel. One does not cancel workshops. The tension affected me in other strange ways. I was just barely pretty enough to be standing before an audience anyway when my left eyebrow began to disappear. Each morning there was less of it and less and less until it was almost all gone. I decided my eyeglasses would hide the blank space, that I could carry on. Then, the morning of the workshop, I arose and looked in the mirror. My eyebrow had reappeared, only this time it was just above my upper lip.

If you are, or plan to be, a public speaker, be prepared to meet a few bumps in the road.

Gender Differences

Despite unisex clothing and hairstyles, despite recurring movements to make women as strong as men and men as sensitive as women, despite every effort to make the two sexes alike, there are subtle differences in the way men and women think, talk, and behave. This is not to say that one is superior to the other. No one in his or her right mind would even hint at anything like that.

There are general differences, though. Observations during the days between Thanksgiving and Christmas reveal many examples of these differences. Most women bake pies, cakes, and cookies. They address cards and shop for gifts. Most men eat pies, cakes, and cookies. They watch football and hunt for game. With glazed eyes, bored men wait and wait in malls while their wives shop and handle all the merchandise in every store.

Men sometimes, though, do go shopping with their wives for the perfect live Christmas tree (folks usually buy a live tree only once in a lifetime). At the tree lot, he buttons his overcoat against the icy wind and points to the first tree he sees. He says, "Honey, do you like this one?" She looks. It's a Charlie Brown tree.

Hiding her horror with a fake smile, she says, "Yes, that's nice, but I like this one." Most women have a natural instinct for aesthetics. They know when a tree is symmetrical.

Wanting to get home to the ball game, he's grateful she's picked one, although he saw nothing wrong with the one he had chosen. He pays the cashier, then struggles mightily to get the ten-footer tied to the top of their small car. He tries to tell the Mrs. the tree will be too tall for their living room. Men usually know more about measurements than women. She says it will be fine.

When they arrive home, he must saw a couple of feet from the bottom, then anchor the tree to its stand. The woman trims the tree while the husband reads the evening paper. When she's finished, sitting not five feet from the tree trimmer, the husband looks around his paper and says, "I didn't know you were trimming the tree. I could have helped."

Not responding, she waits for him to put away the empty boxes that held the trimming and now litter the floor. Oblivious to them, he walks to the kitchen for more snacks. Playing the martyr, she pouts. He watches more football. Tension builds only on her end. She's angry. He's happy. She carries the boxes to the garage. He watches football. Later, he wants to know if he can help put the boxes away. She says nothing, but he can tell she's angry. He's puzzled, wondering what women want anyway.

The next evening, she asks him to put the outside lights around the top of their two-story house. He asks where the lights are.
"In the attic," she says, (where we've stored them for twenty years, she thinks). He asks where the ladder is (in the garage where it's been since we bought the house, she thinks).

He asks where the outdoor extension cords are. They're with the lights, of course. That's a distinguishing characteristic of most men. They can live in a house for years and not know where anything is kept. It's as if, each time, they've just landed from Mars and entered the house for the first time.

Women have their weaknesses, too. Actually, most women never know when the oil in the car needs changing or how to change it if it does. Most women don't know a carburetor from a carbine. They can't repair lamps or replace faucet washers, but they're usually better decorators. If wives aren't careful, husbands will fill a small room with two mammoth pieces of furniture: an ugly brown recliner with arms two feet wide, accompanied by a television with a 37-inch screen. The same sense of proportion or measurement that plays to their advantage on a tree lot or over a workbench totally abandons men inside the house.

Then, there's the unfinished male gene. Almost every man I know has a gene that prevents him from completing a task. If he's helping to fold clothes, he'll leave a few pieces in the dryer. If he's nailing baseboard around a room, he'll leave one small section off. If he's installing an aluminum ceiling over a porch, he'll quit before installing the last strip. It's as if men can't bring themselves to say good-bye to a chore.

Of course, most men don't talk all the time either. In fact, I didn't know my husband could talk until I heard him answer the phone one day and begin talking to a friend he hadn't seen in years. He didn't just talk. He talked with animated expression, as my Sunday school teacher used to say. He talked and talked. That was two years ago; he's said few words since, but there might be another call sometime.

Men don't go wild over teddy bears and Beanie babies, and women aren't obsessed with ball games and chasing animals through the woods. There are differences between men and women, no doubt about it, but I say, "Vive la difference."

Horrorscopes and Crystal Bawls

Most of us are superstitious, although we're loath to admit it because we think of ourselves as enlightened. We consider openly superstitious persons to be unenlightened.   Those who believe in numerology, astrological predictions, crystal balls, black cats, and psychics, though, think of themselves as enlightened, too. Why, we're all as bright as diamonds in the noonday sun.

A friend recently said she believes that three is her lucky number. Eight is mine. I was married on July 18, gave birth to our son in the eighth month, and I was notified of a tenure-track teaching position at a local college on September 18—all watershed events that changed the course of my life.

Our daughter, however, when learning of my lucky number, said,

"What's that make me? Chopped liver? I was born on October 11, no eight about it."

It is difficult to account for that because her birthday was as lucky for me as any day in my life. Superstitions don't hold up well under scrutiny. Still, my belief in eight as a lucky number clings to me like a sticky cobweb. I understand there's a whole body of knowledge on numerology, but I don't want to learn more about it. My activities would halt while I searched to see whether I'd be lucky or unlucky, depending on the number involved. Before taking action, I'd have to consider time, date, and number of persons or movie offers. I'd never do anything but look up numbers to which I have a general aversion anyway.

A year ago, I read a classified ad for an astrological columnist. Honest. If knowing that writers are hired to make predictions about the future doesn't shake your faith in astrology, I don't know what would. Realizing these predictions are as bogus as political candidates' promises to make life marvelous for all, I still read my horoscope when I think about it. I'm a happily married woman with children and grandchildren, but my forecast recently told me that at a party I'd meet a young, handsome lover.

The only experiences I've had with crystal balls occurred years apart. When I was thirteen, my friends and I visited a fortuneteller who had set up a tent near our home. I remember her dark eye shadow and a multicolored scarf tied tight around her head from which dangled large golden loop earrings. She bent over her crystal ball. Moving her hands over it in circular motions, she mumbled words in an unintelligible language. At one point, she bawled. She had long fingers with pointed nails painted dark purple. She said I would marry, live in the country, and have two children. We paid her our money and giggled all the way home. She took our money and laughed all the way to you know where.

Years later, I was on the other side of the crystal ball, creating fictional stories for students at a school carnival. Ironically, I don't remember my attire and what I told them, but I bet they remember. They, too, giggled as they ducked through the small opening to leave the tent where I held court.

You probably don't believe in crystal balls, but do you shudder when a black cat crosses your path? Do you ever knock on wood to ensure continued good luck? Are you wary of Friday 13? If you break a mirror, do you believe you'll have seven years of bad luck? If it's easier to walk under a ladder, do you go around it instead? When I was a child, I tried not to step on sidewalk cracks because I had heard the warning, "Step on a crack and break your mother's back." A bird entering the house and a picture falling off the wall are both omens of impending death. If you drop a dishrag, expect a guest. If you take bread and have bread, expect a hungry visitor. There are hundreds of superstitions we swear we don't believe. Still, we think, why tempt fate? Of course, there are those who believe Elvis is still alive. He's been seen in almost every fast food restaurant in the nation. I was behind a dusty van one morning, and written in the dust were the words, "Follow me. Elvis is in here." I was tempted.

A friend who keeps abreast of the latest news has told me that the new welfare-to-work program is working. Some women who were on welfare have been hired as psychics. If you want to know whether to take that new job or to believe that new heartthrob, just call your friendly psychic. I'm going to call and ask if Elvis is in my part of the country now. Of course, I won't believe her because I'm enlightened.

In Search of Self

"Lost O Lost" is a recurring phrase in one of Thomas Wolfe's novels. Arguably, the phrase is a theme that runs throughout his works. Perhaps, then, Wolfe should be remembered more for his early recognition of the "lost" individuals in America than for his statement "You can't go home again." Of course, there were not nearly as many lost persons in Wolfe's lifetime as there are now.

Why, since the author's death in 1938, the number of Americans who can't find their way has increased to a grand scale, having reached almost epidemic proportions. We know this is true because close observations reveal the many avenues people are pursuing in an effort to find themselves.

I know one man who has changed his name three times and still isn't sure who he is. He does claim to have been a prince in a former life, but as all his friends will quickly tell you, he's no prince now. I think the loss of blue blood has frustrated him, so his search continues. He has recently joined a self-help group, one whose members try to delve into their past lives to see where they've been so they'll know where they are and where they're going. I'm not sure they ever find out who they are, though.

Belonging to an organization or a clique is another way people can achieve some sort of self-image. If they have no notion of who they are or what they stand for, they can always say, "I am a member of the Descendants of Royalty Association." No one admits to belonging to a clique but, nonetheless, clique members have smug feelings, knowing they belong, knowing they are important.

Careers also offer identification. Persons don't have to bother with self-identification beyond saying they are lawyers or accountants or scholars or plumbers or even beach bums.

Slogans and symbols displayed for all the world to see help folks achieve self-description. "Eat more opossum" written on a bumper sticker that, in turn, has been slapped onto the back bumper of an old pickup truck is telling—very. "I'm the Parent of an Honor Student" gives another kind of message, classifying the displayer of the bumper sticker as one proud papa or mama. By the time the kids are grown, though, a new bumper sticker emerges: "We're spending our kids' inheritance." A few retirees tell the world who they are with these bumper stickers stuck to their vehicles that are sometimes new Cadillacs, "No clock. No boss. No money." Some slogans are vulgar; others are aggressive. I saw one recently that said, "Don't start with me." I didn't.

During the Vietnam conflict, T-shirts boasting the peace sign told the world about the wearers. Pricey running shoes—costing about the same today as a good used car in Wolfe's time—tell viewers the wearers buy clothing with big-name labels. Manufacturers adore label-lovers, for the wearers advertise companies' products and, what's more, pay for the privilege. Do you think label-buyers know who they are?

Political campaigns offer opportunities for self-classification. During one presidential election, I saw a woman wearing a porkpie hat covered with slogans and buttons, all proclaiming her political preferences. She wore a red, white, and blue vest also covered with campaign buttons. Then, there are the "eat-more-beef" proponents, contrasted by members of People for the Ethical Treatment of Animals (PETA). There are tree huggers and tree cutters, more classifications that say, "This is who I am." These outward trappings represent only the public face, not the private.

Who are we really? Name changes, organizational memberships, careers, slogans, labels, and politics may define a small part of who we are.

It is how we treat our fellow human beings that really identifies us, especially how we treat our family members and those under us in the hierarchy
at work. Our full character profile, then, is hidden within the dark corners
of our hearts where we harbor either bitterness or love. It is only there,
deep within the human heart where we can discover whether we are lost,
oh, lost.

Industrial Strength

    Carrying clipboards, they wore white coats and serious expres-
sions. They never laughed. There wasn't time. In fact, time itself was the
all-in-all, the very thing that had to be squeezed into a tight little ball. More
and more had to be accomplished in less and less time. Laughter took time
and cost money. The folks in the white coats were efficiency experts, and
one day in a plant where my friend once worked, these time-keepers crawled
all over the place. They watched workers type and push buttons on ma-
chines. They recorded how many seconds each movement took. Workers'
nerves became frayed, but no one had asked employees for suggestions.
    One excellent painter, during his ordeal with the white-cloaked
experts, was timed to see how long it took him to dip his brush in the can
and then remove it. The painter became so nervous he spilled the bucket of
paint all over the place, which probably didn't add much to the study. Time
management would be second only to quality control. Industry was about
to take a new turn. Before that fateful day, my friend says industry was
filled with dedicated people who loved their work and life and laughter.
They had fun and still got the job done. They had the freedom to wax
creative and to go beyond the call of duty. He believes all that has changed.
    He told me a story about an engineer who was recognized as an
expert in flow-measurement problems. The engineer had been working

diligently to solve a problem but had not been able to find the solution. After working hard for a long period of time and even thinking about the problem at home on his own time, he finally solved it. Feeling a great sense of accomplishment, he went back to his desk for a few minutes of deserved rest. Leaning back in his chair with a satisfied smile on his face, he had just placed his feet on his desk when a time-efficiency specialist approached.

The expert asked, "What are you doing?

The engineer replied, "Nothing."

What are you supposed to be doing?"

The engineer said, "Nothing. I just finished a project."

Holding his clipboard in a threatening position, the expert asked, "Don't you look for something else to do when you finish one job?"

The engineer said, "Let me ask you. Does a firefighter go out and set a house on fire just so he can stay busy?"

The expert turned and walked away (hurriedly, of course).

Another day, an analytical group was busy programming gas chromatographs. The group comprised talented and diligent workers who were committed to their jobs in a way that management could never force them to be.

Their supervisor came by one day and said, "We're having New York visitors, and we want you to look busy."

The group took the comment as an insult. They, in turn, went to the mechanic shop and had manacles and chains made. When the visitors walked by, they saw employees manacled and chained to their instruments. These instrumentation specialists were all men who had served in World War II. They were veterans who had endured combat situations, so they didn't get upset when reprimands came their way later. They were, after all, as efficient in industry as they had been in war. They did their jobs, always, no matter what was asked of them. What's more, many worked for their employers on their own time without compensation. They often took work home and completed the job, again, without pay. They did it just for the sake of trying to figure something out. They had a sense of humor. Indeed, humor was the glue that held everything together. It was as important as having the latest technology of the day. This analytical group, with its wit and wisdom, was responsible for developing the application of the gas chromatograph to online process measurement. This process today serves as the method of control in the chemical industry on a worldwide basis.

The kind of commitment leading to this valuable process and to real industrial strength was in place long before the emergence of time experts armed with clipboards. Imagine that.

It Takes Two Villages

Look out! Another study has just been completed—one that claims the biggest complaint of teenagers is that they don't get to spend enough time with their parents. The White House, no less, plans to hold a conference (which may result in a task force, so beware) to see what can be done to provide more quality time for teens and parents to spend together. Now persons who believe that teenagers want to be even in the same village with their old-fashioned, uninformed parents have more faith in studies than I do.

Anyone who has ever lived with or still lives with teenagers will tell you the last thing they want is to be around their parents (unless, of course, the teens need money). Those between twelve and twenty want to be with their own kind, and secretly parents agree. I think it all has something to do with getting ready for the empty-nest syndrome. Teenagers become so annoying to the older generation, including parents, and vice versa, that parents and offspring eagerly part when the time comes. If teens remained as adorable as four-year-olds, we'd never want to let them go. Mother Nature wisely intercedes, so we don't just let go when they leave for college, we celebrate.

So much separates teenyboppers from parents that any time spent together would soon disintegrate into time of the poorest quality. Think about it. Teenagers have hairstyles that parents usually hate, but tolerate to keep shouting matches to a minimum. The father's hair is cut for the office, conservative by any standard. The young boy's hair is either nonexistent in a skinhead style or shaved halfway up his head as if a bowl has served as a guide for the clippers. Of course, his hair might be drooping over his shoulders, hiding the despised earring in the left earlobe.

Clothing further widens the chasm between adolescents and parents. The grunge look must have caused a great deal of anxiety. Boys sometimes still walk around with the crotch of their pants so close to the ground that one wonders how they walk at all. Clothes, though, are important symbols for teens. When older folks wore polyester, teens wore jeans. When older folks discovered the coolness and comfort of jeans, youngsters began to wear polyester.

Then, there's the music. One generation has through the ages ridiculed another generation's music. The Big Band Era gave my family the jitters while my friends and I enjoyed jitterbugging. Today's teen music is so loud that the noise (according to yet another study) has damaged teenagers' hearing. Whereas yesteryear's music—now pejoratively called "elevator music"—was soft and slow, today's music thumps and rocks to a different beat. Yesterday's was mostly romantic; today's is often political.

Language itself throws up yet another barrier. Yesterday's squares are today's geeks. I recently asked a friend who has a teenager to tell me some of the slang teens use today. She said, "I would, but he won't talk to me or his dad." Does that say anything about how much youngsters want to be with their parents?

Finally, there is the difference in hormones. By the time parents have endured sleepless nights with colic and colds, by the time they've coped with kindergarten and recitals and middle school and high school, the flame of their hormones has all but died, leaving little more than pale ashes. Teenagers, however, are just discovering things Mom and Dad wish they'd not yet discover. Hormones come on like gangbusters, and there's little parents can do to slow them down. While Mother and Father, then, believe Johnny and Jenny are studying, they're dreaming of love. Their hormones are, as the cliché goes, raging, raging. All these differences between adolescents and their parents mean one thing: the two generations don't want to be together any more than necessary. The ideal would be two villages—one for teenagers and one for their parents.

June Brides and Lost Grooms

If you want to make the average man feel uncomfortable, force him to wear a tuxedo. If you want to make him feel lost and insignificant and miserable, force him to wear a white or pink tuxedo. June is the stellar month for brides, and grooms have no choice but to go along to get along. From the father of the bride to the groom to the best man to the ushers, men fair poorly in June. It's a time when macho men can be seen wearing boutonnières, ruffles, cummerbunds, and, yes, pink tuxes. June is for brides, but in order to be a bride, she must have a groom. That's where the man enters the picture. Actually, the groom—palely loitering in his pink or white outfit—is there, in part anyway, to make the wedding pictures complete. Like the rest of the wedding party (except the bride in white, of course), he serves to carry out the color scheme that the bride and mother of the bride have chosen.

As soon as the engagement is announced, the bride-to-be seems to undergo a strange kind of metamorphosis in reverse. From a lilting butter-fly, prior to the wedding announcement, she transforms into a consumer as devouring as the caterpillar itself. Driven to shop for wedding trappings, she begins by reading thick bridal magazines. She struggles with choosing just the right colors and flowers and a photographer who will capture every minute of her day. She chooses engraved wedding invitations, lines up bridesmaids, the flower girl, and on and on.

At some point, long before the wedding day, the now full-fledged caterpil-lar drags along her fiancé to the bridal registry where he shifts awkwardly from one Nike-clad foot to the other while she animatedly looks at a thou-sand patterns of china and silverware. She holds in front of him a dainty porcelain cup boasting a mauve flower and asks if he likes it.

Shrugging his drooping shoulders, he mumbles, "It's okay."

He doesn't understand why a coffee mug wouldn't be better than a tiny translucent cup. What's the difference between made in China and made of china, he wonders.   He doesn't want to tell her what he really thinks. In truth, he longs to be on the golf course or in the deep woods where wild turkeys beckon. He's having second thoughts about the forth-coming formal affair but is caught in the tender trap of a June wedding.

Despite all the bride's efforts, her day isn't always perfect. I know one man, an avid sports enthusiast, who had to wear a white tux at his wedding. On the special day, he marched down the aisle, smiling sheepishly. Only later, did his family learn he had worn white basketball socks with his tuxedo. Moreover, they had wide gold stripes at the tops. Another friend, an usher at a June wedding, said his tuxedo was so wrinkled that when he looked in the mirror he looked like a giant carnation. My husband told me about a man who years ago was the father of the bride. He was told to wear a formal black suit. Since he already had a nice black jacket, he shopped just for matching trousers. When he found a pair at an upscale store, they were so expensive for a one-time wearing that he decided to go to a store where he could buy an inexpensive pair, in this case, a cheap pair. Later, as he walked proudly down the aisle with his bride-daughter holding his arm, he suddenly felt cool air hitting the inside of both legs. The inner seam of his pants had come loose, and the sleazy fabric, like Zorro's cape, was flapping in the air-conditioned breeze. The father of the bride was as miserable as the poor groom in his white tux and the ushers in their rose-tinted attire.

The fact is, though, it's not what the wedding party wears during the marriage ceremony; it's how well the marriage wears.

Larger Than Life

The Puritans' holier-than-thou attitude has through the years been expanded to a bigger-than-thou mentality. We can see it in everything from the fast-food chains' bigger burgers, to the Speedy Shop-a-Second's bigger slurps. Grocery chains, not to be outdone in the bigger-is-better craze, have increased the footage of their floor space until we no longer need to climb mountains to get exercise. We can just wend our way up and down miles of aisles in gigantic stores. Exhausted by the time we get to the dairy products and eggs, we find that large eggs are really small compared to extra large and jumbo size. For older shoppers who cannot endure the long-distance marathon required, stores provide electronic carts. Young shoppers would like to ride in them, too, but know the carts are not for them. Grocery chains—pressed with the need to fill all that space with something—now contain everything from florist shops to pharmacies to delicatessens to magazine sections, but where's the beef? Why, it's in the back of the store; just walk two miles down aisle 13. The store of yester-year was tiny, but all the shopper had to do was hand an order to the clerk across a counter filled with penny candy. The clerk did all the shopping for the customer while the two chatted about the latest church social or the suspicious-looking stranger in town. It was a warm and personal experience.

Today, movie theaters have wrap-around screens where faces twenty feet tall overpower us. And there is not just one theater under a single roof; there are at least half a dozen. Refreshments at the movies include candy bars as big as breadboxes. Popcorn is sold in half-gallon buckets of cardboard. Gigantic movie treats have price tags to match. They are large enough to make a down payment on a small house, but there are few small houses being built anymore.

Everything just continues to grow and grow. Most new homes today are as mammoth as hotels. I know of several recently constructed houses that boast more than one kitchen, although I can't imagine why. Rooms can have at least eighteen-foot ceilings, and there are countless baths and halls and niches and rooms everywhere. We need a compass to find our way through these enormous domiciles. Closets in new dwellings are often larger than living rooms in older homes. Soaking tubs and hot tubs get bigger and bigger. Gigantic television screens can cover half a wall while the quality of TV programs continues to diminish.

Vehicles have been getting more massive, too. One couple who looked at a home we had on the market a few years ago wanted to buy our house, but their car was too long for our garage. Sports utility vehicles—already under fire by those who don't have to drive off snowy hills in the winter—are longer and wider. Eighteen-wheelers, already colossal, have almost doubled in length as they piggyback their way down our highways. We watch in amazement as they pass us like wide trains on large rubber wheels.

Cruise ships, as titanic as small towns, can transport thousands of passengers. They offer huge pools and tennis courts and long tables filled with tantalizing foods. Passengers are pampered and entertained aboard ships with more decks and cabins than a centipede has legs.

Part of the problem with everything getting more and more massive is that advertisers—those word wizards—have trouble trying to come up with new adjectives to tell us just how big big can be. They've depleted the current modifiers and have resorted to words like biggie and jumbo. In the meantime, we go to the movies where we gaze up at the giant screen, place a jumbo bucket of popcorn on our biggie bellies and notice how everyone is getting, um, bigger—that is everyone except us.

Mad Scientists' Warnings

Late August sun slanted through our kitchen window, revealing billions of tiny dust particles. Ignoring them while preparing breakfast, I was forced to ask my husband what at first blush might seem like a strange question.

"Bill," said I, "which exit would you like to use to depart this world? As I see it, you have three choices: margarine, butter, or neither."

I explained to him that a club for dieters had discovered we must eat at least a little butter or margarine each week; otherwise, we'll be doomed. Butter has been on Dr. Frankenstein's bad list for a long time because of its cholesterol-producing properties, but it has finally submitted to a new study indicating that margarine is the real killer. There you have it: a, b, or c. Any one of these seems like a deadly choice to me.

Contradictions by scientists or other kinds of experts have by now become commonplace. Even the apple-a-day maxim was transformed into a horror story a few years back when the Alar™ (daminozide) scare came to the forefront. A later study indicated we could again eat apples to keep the doctor away; in fact, we should. Cranberries, coffee, artificial sweeteners, red meat, chicken, and even fish, in various studies, have all been linked in mysterious ways to carcinogens. Later studies indicate we should ignore the earlier studies. Are you confused yet? Stressed yet?

Anything grilled over charcoal is out—for now anyway. Scientific studies have long indicated that tea is a mild carcinogen. Mild? Ah, but have you heard the latest study on tea drinking, especially green-tea drinking? The health gurus and scientists are giving green tea four-star reviews for its cancer-fighting polyphenols. Why, its antioxidant, epigallocatechin-gallate (EGCG) is more than 100 times greater than that found in vitamin E, which is important to know. Before buying a truckload of green tea, though, you might want to wait for the next study.

Sugar is labeled white poison by many food guards, those white-coated detectives who stand watch over our well-being. Both aspartame and sugar, then, must be avoided, which leaves life pretty sour when you think about it. Some diet specialists recommend low-fat consumption; another group's study indicates our food pyramid is upside down, meaning we're fat-deprived. (I rather like the latter study.) By the way, my husband has conducted his own study, which found that anything labeled "fat-free" really means you should just as well eat the package and throw the food away. The package will taste better.

I knew if we waited long enough sugar would be back, and with a vengeance. Chocolate has long been considered bad for us because of its high fat content, not to mention the amount of sugar it must contain to make it edible. Guess what? Chocolate is now good for us. I'm not sure why, and I'm not about to ask. Here's notice to all chocoholics. Have at it before another study is done.

Like the studies themselves, the egg has been incredible for a long time. In fact, we've been programmed to think of eggs as pure cholesterol. Now, we're told that's not true, that they're really good for us. We're not convinced, though. The scientists waited too long between studies on the egg.

Of course, all fruits and vegetables sprinkled with insecticides are bad for us, as are all foods with additives. I think this includes all foods. Milk and tap water are to be avoided, but wine (now, now, just a sip a day) can be good for us according to studies that alcoholics would love. Yuppies made bottled water as fashionable as cell phones and pagers. The general population now buys small plastic bottles of spring water by the cartons. They should watch those plastic containers. According to the latest studies, however, bottled water is no different from tap water, and in some cases, contains harmful bacteria that chlorine has zapped in tap water. The moral: don't drink water.

Apparently, despite lengthening life spans, we live in a world fraught with dangers and not just from the food we eat and the liquids we drink. Deer, when they're not jumping onto the hoods of our moving vehicles, are transporting tiny ticks that cause Lyme disease. Air bags in our vehicles, once considered life-saving devices, can now spring forward and smash into us with the same force as a crash into a concrete building at 80 miles per hour. The study indicating this new hazard came out just a few weeks after we traded in our old car for one with air bags. For years, we've been told to use sunblock or, better still, stay out of the sun as much as possible. Now, we're told that sun is good for us.

The very air we breathe is not safe. Poor smokers must huddle in zero weather outside buildings while feeding their insatiable appetite for yet another cigarette. Passive smoke will not be tolerated because studies have shown. . . . Well, you know the rest. As for the smokers and their demise, cigarettes are slower than pneumonia.

What with acid rain, depletion of the ozone layer, overhead powerlines, cell phones, radon, and those ever-present dust mites with their waste products, we don't dare eat, drink, or breathe, much less be merry. Of course, we can always wait for the next study.

Martha Stewart Christmas

Our daughter tells me that Martha Stewart makes her own snowflakes, and according to a canned e-mail message, she even lays her own Fabergé eggs. I'm not sure about the latter, but I do know if you can imagine it, Martha can make it. While creating something flawless, she simultaneously wears high-heeled shoes, a gorgeous outfit, and a casual hairstyle that must require a special artistry. Her greatest creation, however, is one cool billion dollars plus. The morning after the announcement of her waking as a billionaire, Martha couldn't stop smiling on the *Today* show. Her husband, whose timing we can all identify with, had recently divorced her or she divorced him. I didn't know, then, whether her perpetual grin was due to the loss of husband or the increase of wealth.

Regardless of gender, folks everywhere have stopped snickering at her fanatical preoccupation with getting bed linens and towels to match, of setting the perfect table with home-made, hand-dipped candles glowing amid holly (home-grown, of course), of her ability to create anything at anytime and anywhere with a minimum of materials. Give her a pine cone, and she can create, well, a billion dollars.

Observing this cultural phenomenon, I decided to create my own Martha Stewart Christmas. Like all prissy perfectionists, I'm going to pass along my experiences during my trip into Martha's fantasy land.

First, carve out large blocks of time. It will help if you have a chef, several gardeners, landscape artists, maids, personal shoppers, decorators, and the like. If you can't afford these, don't despair. I discovered you could forgo sleep and work all night. Remember, though, to smile pleasantly regardless of fatigue, stress, and nasty barbs aimed at you by imperfect, jealous friends.

I began shopping for my Martha makings after I looked at an eighteen-inch plastic tree in a flower shop. The price tag was $95 (honest). I had an old tree of the same size at home, so I reasoned that I could redecorate it and get a brass container to hide the rustic stand. Like Martha, I would make my own tiny velvet bows with which I would adorn the tree. I would have my own priceless creation.

For the first time in my life, I browsed through the craft department. It was a shock. There were no brass containers, only small cardboard boxes of various shapes and sizes, and they were waiting to be painted or trimmed with I knew not what. The word faux as in false came to mind. Desperate, I walked past a large supply of pipe cleaners and knew someone had meant to shelve them with the pipes but had goofed. I searched for spray paint, but it was sold out to creators who knew to shop early for such items. Not to worry, though. I found small bottles of gold paint. Savvy, I knew to buy sealer for the cardboard box I bought.

A few hours later, long after my Martha smile had disappeared, I struggled at the kitchen table in an effort to make my tree impeccable. I was off to a poor start. The bow making was not going well. I attached the first bow, which was so large and clunky, it hid the upper half of the small tree. Besides, the huge square knot that should have been hidden in the back was showing. Shucks. Also, I had forgotten to buy a paint brush. Feeling resourceful, though, I used a paper towel to paint the box. When the paint dried, my box looked like a golden porcupine. Lint from the paper towel had stuck in the paint. I tossed the whole thing in the trash, but I'm not one to give up easily.

I moved on to cookie baking, an activity at which virtually every woman excels. I measured ingredients and refrigerated large bowls of sticky dough. The time came for the creative part. I was ecstatic. I removed the first bowl and divided the dough in half. A large clump stuck to the board. I added flour. The dough still stuck to my hands and the board and the rolling pin. I added more flour and finally rolled my dough to about one-fourth inch thick. I cut out Christmas trees, Santa faces, sleighs, and Christmas stockings. Wow! I was doing it. As I placed the cookies in the oven, my Martha smile had returned. Seven minutes later, baked cookies waited to be iced and decorated. Then a thought occurred to me. Perhaps I should taste one. I bit down but not through the cookie. Later, as I watched through the kitchen window to see if the squirrels could eat my cookies, I discovered they couldn't bite through them either. No wonder Martha Stewart smiles. She has it all over me.

Members of the Bored

It is the little things that make up the whole of life. Each day is filled with, well, trivia. In other words, Trivial Pursuit isn't just a game; it defines who we are. Occurring only a few times in a lifetime are the big events—events like weddings, divorces (the two being almost a hyphenated term these days), births, deaths, and cures for diseases. Try to remember the last time a cure instead of a profitable ongoing treatment was discovered. What all this means is that we tend to talk about the mundane, the ordinary, and in so doing, we bore our listeners. Since I haven't written a how-to piece for you, I'm going to do that now. I thought you might enjoy learning how to be a bore. If you do the opposite, though, you can avoid transforming your friends into members of the bored.

Here are a few tips. Tell every detail of your ordinary day. Recite what you had for breakfast, bite by bite. This is also a good time to discuss your favorite foods and your least favorite. With luck, you can keep your listener bored for hours. If you didn't sleep the night before, be sure to mention that. Your listener is waiting with baited breath to hear about your night. Yeah, right.

If you did sleep, you still have an opportunity to bore listeners until their eyes cross and their mouths drool. Tell everything that happens in your dreams. If you dreamed you zoomed across the sky in a golden chariot lined with purple velvet, and below earthbound admirers bowed to you, tell everyone in earshot. If you're one of those rare creatures who dream of flying, tell it. Tell it. Recounting dreams is a sure-fire way of putting your audience to sleep. An aside: members of the bored can sleep with their eyes wide open.

Discuss the number of pills you take for each ailment, and whatever else you do, talk about your illnesses. When someone asks how you are, that's your cue to launch into a long list of afflictions, and don't forget the details. If you work at it, you can talk longer about your operation than the time you spent in the operating room. In my grammar-writing book, *The Confident Writer*, I address this very problem. Should you use well or good when someone asks you how you feel? My advice here is to avoid worrying about this rule because listeners don't really want to know how you feel even if they ask. The asking is all a part of the meaningless prattle we humans engage in every day. It's like talking about the weather when we have nothing else to say. The way we spend our days is the way we spend our lives.

Do you have children or grandchildren? Ah, that's good. With grandchildren, you might even be elected chairperson of the bored. Talk about how clever they are, how beautiful and perfect and intelligent. Share every statement they've ever made. If you have babies, you can discuss their, well, bodily functions, especially if you're dining with childless friends. And don't forget the pictures. Carry a pound or two of your children's or grandchildren's photos. Corner friends where they can't escape; then show every snapshot, commenting at length on each one.

If you don't have children, you're still in luck. You can be one of today's instant experts by giving lots of advice on child rearing. Start each statement by saying, "If that were my child. . . ." You get the gist. Soon, you can whip those pathetic parents in line, those parents who have never heard of the word discipline.

If you want to see your friends' eyes turn blank, speak endlessly about people your friends don't know. Again, it's important to remember details. If that doesn't work—but I'm sure it will—show your vacation videos. Run hours and hours of videos showing ocean waves breaking on a sandy shore. In the background are tiny specks of people no viewer could possibly recognize. If you don't have videos, vacation snapshots will bore in the same way photos of grandchildren bore.

If all this fails, you can simply dominate the conversation, talking on and on about yourself. If your listener tries to say something, speed up. If your listener does get to talk, don't listen. Think about what you're going to say next.

Finally, to be a thoroughbred bore, don't read books and don't keep up with current events. Live in your own little cocoon, oblivious to the world around you. That should do it. I'll bet you could add to my list because there is no end to trivia in our daily lives.

Mother Tongue

Creatively reshaping expressions, Annie Dillard's mother provided inspiration that led the author to a lifelong love of language and, more than likely, to the writing of captivating essays and books.

My mother's word contortions have inspired me, too, but she works from the opposite end of the language spectrum—that is, she unwittingly reshapes words and expressions. My mother speaks the Appalachian dialect fluently, as well as confidently and proudly. A colorful dialect it is. Actually, she often displays her own idiolect, creating unusual words as she speaks. For instance, I asked her one year to attend an education rally with me in our state's Capitol. We needed as many warm bodies as possible to show support for higher education. My mother was willing to go with me. She did not promise rapt attention, however, and after a few minutes at the rally, she wrote the following note to me: "When can we go home? I'm not one bit insterned in this." She had created a new word by blending interested and concerned. Obviously, she was neither.

Another day when I was visiting her, she showed me a new recipe she had written on an index card; it was a recipe a friend had dictated by phone. I read the words in Mother's neat handwriting. "Sprinkle a little time on the feesh." My mom's handwritten grocery orders befuddle my husband when he occasionally shops for her. Scott's toilet paper is Scoot's t.p. Instead of peaches, she writes pichus.

Her pronunciations of many words frequently need translations. She pronounces fish the way she spells it. President Bush is President Boosh, and cushion is always cooshun. Battery is battry, and so it goes. By the use of spoonerisms, malapropisms, and other linguistic –isms, my mom has made me aware of the versatility of our language.

Recently, she and I took a walk through the woods near my country home. In the far distance, we could barely hear a neighbor's radio as it pounded out a country song. Mom tripped along to the tune, turned her head toward me and said, "Do you know that Wammy Tynette is my favorite singer?"

I said, "You mean Tammy Wynette."

She rolled her eyes at her smart-aleck daughter and said, "Whatever."

As we continued talking though the woods, she asked, "Did I ever tell you about poor Grace who lives in our apartment building?"

I said, "What about poor Grace?"

She said, "Well, she's been having lots of bladder problems. She finally got so bad they had to take her to the hospital and have her castrated."

"Mom, do you mean catheterized?" asked I.

She replied testily, "No, I mean what I say. A nurse who knows everything told me about it. She should know. She also told me when you have any disease that ends in -itis, you have some kind of information."

"Mom, that's inflammation, isn't it?" I asked.

My tag question clearly showed my own lack of confidence around my mother, confidence that as far as I know she's never lacked.

"Whichever," she said. "Anyway, if she hadn't made that trip to the hospital, she'd been up a tree without a paddle."

"Right," said I.

She then told me about an incident that happened in her apartment building.

"We had some excitement in the lobby the other day. A young man came in and stole some money from the petty cash box in the office. They called the poleeces, and they came and took that young man out on the sidewalk and fondled him."

"Mom," I said, "they what?"

She said, "Well, you're in English. They wanted to see if he had a knife or gun on him."

"You mean frisked," I offered timidly.

She looked at me in dismay. "No, honey. That's horse of another feather. You want to watch your language."

"Right," I said softly.

The music in the background thumped out a new tune, and I knew the future would hold many newly formed words for me to ponder. Like Dillard, I, too, have been inspired by the mother tongue.

On the Bright Side

Laughing, my daughter said, "Perhaps they should hold the Mayo."

She has a great sense of humor. Her comment was triggered by Mayo Clinic's latest study. According to Mayo, if we look on the bright side of things instead of whining and complaining and criticizing and on and on, we'll live a good 19 percent longer and, apparently, be happier doing it. I have a friend who is delighted to tell me again and again how she's outlived three husbands and is working on a fourth. She's eighty-three and continues to look on the bright side of life.

Instead of looking at the old tumbler as half empty, then, you know how we should view it if we want to extend life. These results raise a few questions though. How do we account for all those mean-spirited grouches who have reached the hundred mark and beyond but continue to find fault with everything and everyone? Also, I'm not quite sure how Mayo's study is going to mesh with one conducted at Yale, the results of which were announced first.

A psychology professor at Yale conducted a study on how people are affected when they have bad-hair days. Both men and women were included. The results are alarming—although not surprising—for those of us who have had to show up for work with a bump in our hair that couldn't be flattened no matter what or with our hair looking like a starburst. The results indicate that on those nasty-hair days, men have low self-esteem (don't you love that ragged hyphenated expression?), and women fare no better. As far as I know, the professor has not conducted a study on those with no hair versus those with bad hair. Anyway, if we juxtapose the Mayo and Yale studies, we can readily see that bad-hair days could do more than lower our self-esteem. Those gray days could even shorten our lives—that is, unless we can learn to laugh at our hair the way others might snicker behind our backs. It's all a matter of optimism over pessimism.

Learning this, I thought of several incidents that would require a special effort to remain on the sunny side of defeat. I read recently about a sixth grader whose parents sued the school (are you ready?) for losing his Pokemon cards. Can you imagine the extra effort it must take for the teacher, the principal, and the administrators to see the humorous side of this situation?

Yet another experiment revealed that those folks who are most competent at their jobs—who know a great deal, comparatively speaking—have the least self-esteem. Conversely, those who are the least competent are downright cocky. They have all the answers to the world's problems. Do you know anyone like this? Most of us wouldn't have needed a study for this one. The more we learn, the more we know how little we know. That's a fact.

My next example deals with animals. A veterinarian said on *Good Morning America* that we should brush our pets' teeth. He held a toothbrush with a long handle (that's the good news). It was designed for brushing a dog's or cat's teeth. Now, I've had dogs and cats and ducks and chickens as pets all my life and have apparently been a miserable failure at pet ownership because I have never brushed a single pet's teeth. Of course, with the chickens and ducks, I was okay. We now have a stray dog, Freddie

Flealoader. He has two long tushes (my mother's word for eyeteeth), each of which is about an inch long. He's a big dog with big teeth. Although he's friendly, I can't imagine what he would do if I tried to brush his teeth. The vet declares he and I would bond if I would just try, though. I have to think about that. Do I really want to bond to that dog and be super-glued to him everywhere I go? Also, I have a cat named Elizabeth Tailless. Her mate, Richard Burden, went to cat heaven due to kidney failure. We could have called him Cat from Well (excuse the misspelling of that last word). I would have been logically challenged had I tried to brush his teeth and keep my sense of humor at the same time. He was big, too, with claws, when extended, as long as Freddie's "tushes." You can see that there are many events in life that try our good nature, but if we persist on keeping our hearts loving and our eyes smiling, we can live all of 19 percent longer. I hope Mayo's right.

Mirror, Mirror, Who's the Barest of Them All?

Every spring, millions of us are drawn to the *Annual Academy Awards Presentation*, a televised program that demonstrates my mother's maxim in reverse. Before launching into one of her tales, Mom always begins by saying, "To make a short story long. . . ." When those coveted Oscars are presented to movie stars—stars who sometimes wear little more than their symbolic ribbons—we discover just how long producers can make a short story. Although one year's program was supposed to be cut to only—only?—three and a half hours, traditionally, the programs have run for at least four hours. By the end of all the thank-you speeches in which too many stars thank too many persons, by the end of skits, musical performances and chitchats, we feel as if the program has run at least four days. Of course, you must be thinking that we have the option of turning off the television or switching channels. Not so fast. Those clever folks keep us waiting until the last few minutes to see if we've guessed correctly which movie has been the least worst of the season and which two superstars will carry home Oscars for best acting.

While Hollywood's winners smile and hoist their Oscars high into the air, the losers applaud, smile, and pretend they're happy for the winners. Secretly, they're thinking how unfair the selection process must have been or else they would have won, hands down. It's all a matter of pretense from Tinseltown, a magical place renowned for its pretense. While on Oscar night many of the humanitarian stars wear their reminder ribbons for various causes for the world to see, they set examples for the young by smoking cigarettes in their movies. Go figure, as one of my young friends says.

I have another wise friend who claims viewers don't watch the "Oscars" to see who wins anyway. He says they watch to see whether each actress will be able to cross the stage without losing her dress. He sheepishly adds that it doesn't much matter in some cases because the dresses are, well, barely there. He swears each female entertainer stands in front of a long oval mirror before Awards night, looks at herself in her borrowed designer dress, and chants: "Mirror, mirror off the wall/Who's the barest one of all?" If the mirror names another actress as being the barest one of all (so claims my friend), the star goes into a rage, then chooses another dress. This one will expose more midriff, more back. Its neckline will plunge down, down beyond the belly button, and it will boast a slit from its floor-length hemline to the upper thigh.

Every year, movie stars serve as walking advertisements for designers like Dior, Givenchy, Valentino, Armani, and the late Versace. During the 57th Annual Academy Awards, Cher sported a Bob Mackie creation with a headdress that looked like an exploding black widow spider. In keeping with the theme, whatever it was, Mackie covered Cher's throat and, uh, chest with ebony spider-webbing. Only Cher could pull that one off (no pun intended). Whoopi Goldberg served as host at one year's Awards (the 71st presentation ceremony). With her unique sense of humor, she wore a Queen Elizabeth I costume. She came on stage, smiled sweetly, and said, "Welcome. I'm your virgin queen."

There are as many reasons for watching the *Annual Academy Awards Presentation* as there are viewers. I watch because it's live (mostly). I wait, then, to see who's going to fall or streak across the stage (as one man did in 1974, upstaging poor David Niven), or who might do a few pushups (as gray-haired Jack Palance did after winning his Oscar). I watch to see who's going to make the next social gaffe. Most of us recognize the phony face of O-S-C-A-R—phoniness revealed in ribbon-wearing along with ciga-rette-smoking, phoniness revealed in fake smiles alongside bitter disap-pointment. Still, we're drawn to watch because we know stars, like us, are just humans with human flaws. We watch because on Oscar night stars are in roles playing themselves with their flaws and much more exposed.

Phony Phone

"Sorry, I'm in a meeting. Please leave a message at the tone." It's called voice mail, and it's replaced the secretary whose title begins with "secret." The secretary knew how to keep secrets, too. Screening calls for the boss, the efficient assistant with wide-eyed guilt usually said some-thing like, "Mr. Covert is unavailable, but I'll give him your message." There was never a promise that Mr. Covert would return your call. Still, if you had the persuasive skills, the secretary was human and, therefore, sus-ceptible. You had a chance of success.

Technology has replaced the secretaries' carefully worded responses to phone calls. When we call a business office these days and a live human being answers, we feel almost as good as if we had won a million-dollar lottery, one event being about as rare as the other. Even something as simple as trying to get a prescription filled is an exercise in frustration. Since negative connotations have clung to the word "drug," drug stores are now referred to as pharmacies, so I called my pharmacy recently to get a prescription filled. From the miracle of technology came a recorded male voice that was so friendly and articulate that for a fleeting instant I thought I was talking to a thinking person.

The voice said, "Welcome to Technology Pharmacy. Press one if you are a doctor. Press two if you wish to get a prescription filled. Press three if you wish to know the status of a prescription. Press four for pharmacy hours. Press five if you wish to speak to a pharmacist " (no longer a druggist). I hung in there and pressed all the right buttons and then was cut off. Dismayed, I listened to the dreary drone of the dial tone. I tried again and again as the day wore on. Finally, after a long time, I managed to get through and enter all the right information, which resulted in a phony thanks by a voice without heart or brain. Understand that I had not really been thanked at all because only humans know how to thank other humans.

Both homes and businesses have access to a little device known as Caller ID. Ah-ha! That takes the place of the secretary (who is now an administrative assistant, which is another story). We can simply look at the window on the little ID box, and if it's slanted just the right way in the light, we might be lucky enough to see the caller's name, phone number, and date and time of call. If it's a cell-phone call or a pesky marketing person or a sales rep, we see the word "unavailable," which is usually something to avoid, but not always. Most of those cell calls are worth taking, but they, too, display "unavailable" on the ID box. There are pitfalls everywhere in the field of technology.

The sales representatives who peddle recorded music for business phones are surprisingly successful, given the fact that most callers would just as soon enjoy a few minutes of rare silence in an otherwise hectic, noise-polluted world. Of course, I'm guessing, but I'll bet a study would confirm my assertion. What's more, the tunes rocking and thumping their way over phone lines may not match the callers' tastes, but the only choices callers have are to listen or give it up. Ever more clever, these technological wizards are now incorporating advertising chatter along with music as callers patiently wait for that honest-to-life human on the other end.

Then, take call waiting. Please take it. If your call has come into a home first, and you're in deep conversation (be it ever so trivial), you still have the floor. Nonetheless, if another call comes in on the other end, you're put on hold. I have a friend who gives the person on the other end exactly ten seconds after which he hangs up. Wow! I wish I had that kind of courage. I don't. I pretend it's okay that I'm less important than whoever may be calling, even if it's a stranger selling grave plots or house siding or magazines.

Unlisted numbers hide those folks who want to stay undercover. Soon, though, they give their phone numbers out to a select few, a practice that depresses phone company officials. Since we can't keep secrets, those unlisted numbers are quickly listed in phone users' little electronic day planners and even on the backs of grocery lists and coasters. Next thing you know, those undercover folks are as out in the open as the rest of us.

Not all technology is bad. In fact, most of it is good, some better for one group than for others. Repeat dialing is especially useful for political candidates who can call those 900 numbers to vote repeatedly for themselves. Think of all the time they save by not dialing each time they vote. Then there's the MUTE button for times when you want to talk about the person on the other end and don't want him or her to hear you. The MEMORY button is handy for folks who can't remember names and numbers and places and where they put their coffee. If they can just remember that number one is for Aunt Mary and number two is for Uncle Jed, they have it made. Oh, they also must remember to press MEMORY first. Come to think of it, this button may not be too helpful for forgetful folks. I have a button titled FLASH on my phone, and I don't dare push it. I can't imagine what it's for, but some technological wizard decided I needed it. I'll have to get out the instruction book, but that's another story altogether.

Quest for the Fountain of Youth

Space Cowboys, a movie featuring four old men who blast off into space, has inspired me to act and look young again. If you remember John Glenn, you know the movie has imitated life, more or less. *Modern Maturity* and television commercials do not reflect real life. They nonetheless have continued to fan the flame of my desire to be young. *Modern Maturity*, a magazine featuring old folks who can cook light, write books, climb mountains, swim oceans, and dance the night away, has increased my desire to return to those fresh, green days of innocence. I want to go back to the time when I thought mostly of my appearance if, indeed, I thought at all. I want to return to the time when I could dance all night and look good in the process—that is, when I still had a flat tummy, full lips, a smooth face, bright eyes, and shiny black hair.

If I'm to believe the television commercials, I could trip the light fantastic all night just by taking Viagra. Have you ever noticed how, after one little pill, all those folks continue to smile as they dance and dance and dance? I'm sure, then, it's a medication that will make us dance. Maybe Centrum Silver would be a better choice because the young-looking old couple, vitamin enriched, skip across slick rocks embedded in running streams. The couple wear walking shorts and hiking boots as they hold hands and fairly float across rushing water. Then, after hiking through hill and dale all day, they sit by a campfire, smiling and staring wistfully into each other's eyes while sipping steaming coffee from heavy mugs. Ah, youth. How we in America love youth.

To appear young, I could begin by consulting a body-piercing expert. If I'm going to be youthful, I'll have to get with it. Today, I see teenagers with earrings in their navels, noses, and tongues. A piercing person would have trouble getting to my belly button, though, since it's buried in an inch-deep well, and my pug nose would hardly support one earring, much less three. My tongue is off limits, too, because it's strictly functional. I'll have to resort to something else to recapture elusive youth.

Since improving the tummy is out—I refuse to take exercises and give up desserts in the same lifetime—I'll move on to lips. As you know, our lips grow thinner and thinner with the passage of time until, in old age, they're little more than a faint line curving downward on each side. I could see about collagen injections, but after watching a movie star whose lips, after collagen, covered most of her bottom face, I'll steer clear of that.

There are all sorts of products available for helping to reduce fine wrinkles. The weasel word in TV commercials is helping. This means that, despite the satin-skinned teenybopper advertising the product, if you have fine wrinkles and use the product, you'll still have wrinkles until Father Time transforms them into deep ditches. Then, even Retin-A, the ingredient that causes the skin to swell and flatten out wrinkles, won't help.

With respect to bright eyes, contact lenses come in a variety of colors if your eyes aren't too dry to accept them. Mine are, but my white-streaked hair can be solved with a product that tells me I'm worth it.

When I think about those guys in *Space Cowboys*, I know they look old, but they have the right stuff anyway. As I gaze at a photograph of Georgia O'Keeffe, the famous painter, I see the image of an old woman. Still, she is as beautiful as the attitude of the men in *Space Cowboys*. I've decided to remain in the autumn of my life and enjoy it to the fullest, to make my own attitude beautiful.

Reflections on a Winter Night

On winter nights in the country, after the lights are out and our house is wrapped in darkness like black velvet, a silence ensues. Unlike in the city, there are no traffic noises, no ambulance sirens, no people talking, no warning whistles from chemical plants, and no coal-laden barges moving over inky waters. Sometimes, though, I can hear the howling wind and imagine drifts of snow moving through the darkness, or I can hear the faint bark of a dog in the far distance. I listen as the rhythmic clicking on and off of the furnace works to keep our home warm. Mostly, though, there is a silence that, as a song says, paradoxically has sounds of its own. It speaks of a slowing down, of a time for reflection.

We are close to nature in the country, aware of each season's characteristics. At winter's onset, long after the mums have turned brown and the robins have left, I watch for the first snow birds or juncos to land on our deck where they eat leftovers from the suet cake—crumbs dropped by titmice, black-capped chickadees, and woodpeckers. With the appearance of the juncos, I know that snow can't be far behind. Varied and fascinating in other seasons, the landscape in winter is leveled with uniformity under a thick coat of quiet snow. These are some of the changes winter brings.

There are also changes in the seasons of human behavior. Changes, we are told, are as inevitable as sunrise and sunset. I suppose. Conducting research for an article, I recently visited a high school with a sterling reputation and excellent teachers. While there, I was reminded of how the school environment had been altered from that of my school days. It was just before Christmas break. Many employees wore shirts adorned with various holiday messages. Painted on the shirts were pictures of snowmen, holly, bells, sleighs, and Santas. Poinsettias sat on desks and sparkling lights hung along the walls down one hall. All these additions spoke quietly of Christmas, but there were no symbols, no words, no signs of Christ. Those would have been forbidden. Separation of church and state had to be maintained. I know that when schools now offer Christmas plays, they must be careful to omit any mention of Christ lest they be accused of combining state and religion. These are enormous changes that have occurred since I attended the public schools. Then, local communities set policies for their own schools. I'm not making judgments, for the word judgmental has also come under fire.

The students were articulate and seemingly bright, but some were not turning in assignments. They were failing, but felt good about themselves. That was obvious from their quick answers and glib comments. They were steeped in self-esteem, but I knew that unless they were jarred out of their complacency they would one day be unable to get jobs, to earn decent livings. Self-esteem grows from the inside out, not from the outside in.

Another change in today's world includes the ubiquitous use of the word multiculturalism. We talk of multiculturalism, on the one hand, and yet veneer our society with sameness, on the other. For instance, we wish one another happy holidays instead of Merry Christmas or Happy Hanukkah or Happy Kwanza so we don't offend those of different faiths. Certainly, no one wants to do that. I don't.

During the silence of one winter night, I thought of how I would react if someone wished me Happy Hanukkah. I wouldn't be offended. Rather, I would thank that person for the good wishes and explain that I did not celebrate Hanukkah. I would, in turn, wish my Jewish acquaintance Happy Hanukkah. As I listened that night to the icy wind shaking the bare-boned tree limbs, I knew my Jewish friends and associates would not be offended either should I make the social gaffe of wishing them a Merry Christmas. Under the generic happy-holiday greeting, whether written or spoken, we've conformed ourselves into one mold, while at the same time, touting our diverse society. We live in a time of contradictions not easily reconciled.

Later, during the velvet blackness of another hushed night, I wondered if we, like my house, have been wrapped in a strange kind of darkness, a darkness with a subsequent silence that has a message all its own. We listen but do not hear.

Road to Utopia

You know how you're treated when, in the market for a new car, you first enter a showroom at a dealership. The sales rep gives your every desire, your every question, your every concern the greatest attention. In short, you're treated like royalty. Nothing is too good for you. You're offered coffee, maybe even cookies. You're invited to take that under-the-lights shiny red convertible for a test drive. You're told to take as long as you like, but once on the road, you discover the tank has only a half-gallon of gasoline. Despite treatment fit for a king or queen, you nonetheless harbor an inexplicable feeling of uneasiness.

During each even-numbered fourth year, we endure a major election year. Your treatment by candidates eager to get votes is similar to sales reps eager to get commissions. Just for the record, I support the system. Strange as it is, it somehow works. Still, I recognize the pitfalls. Recently, I attended a meet-the-candidates gathering. Entering the school gym was much like entering a new-car showroom. I haven't felt so loved and cherished and honored since we bought our silver-plum automobile. I was hugged and adored. I was the recipient of smiles and coffee and cookies and pamphlets and plans. For that one fleeting evening, I was important. I was somebody. I was, er, empowered, for I was a potential vote for each enthusiastic contender. Candidates were eager to hear my concerns, wishes, and questions. Ready solutions and answers were forthcoming. I knew we were all on the road to Utopia.

Candidates or their representatives had only ninety seconds in which to tell us why we should cast our votes for them. Many boasted about being third- and fourth-generation residents of our county. They told us how many children they had and who their wives were. By golly, if the candidates themselves were not long-time residents, then their wives and their wives' families were, which I guess was almost as good. Some told us about their present jobs or about coaching various sports or volunteering in various organizations. As precious seconds ticked away, I wondered why those factors should warrant my vote, especially since I've been in the area only eight years, making me a new-comer, still an outsider. A few—too few—told us what they hoped to accomplish for our state, for our area.

A few candidates promised to ensure that folks in the southern part of our county would have greater access to city water. They promised improved roads. They promised that the area in which I live would get a sewage system. Incredibly, we have no sewage system. If all this happens soon, we might even move into the 20th century now that we're already in the 21st. That would be good. I came away from the meeting, then, with the ability to put faces with names. I came away with a better understanding of the few candidates' positions—that is, the positions of the few who had explained them. I love meet-the-candidates events, partly because I like being queen for an evening.

Television commercials during political camp-pains are slicker—not necessarily better—just slicker. Usually, some out-of-state public relations firm gets millions of dollars to create television commercials that make each local hopeful look simultaneously like a highbrow and a low-brow—that is, a country bumpkin or good ole boy, a task so difficult it's probably worth the money. According to TV ads, one candidate is going to make our schools safer and get free prescription drugs for senior citizens and improve education and improve nursing-home care and lower taxes and decrease crime and upgrade the infrastructure. If he gets elected, he's going to be one busy office holder. He has spent more money in his bid for office than most West Virginians earn in a lifetime, but if he sends a letter to my husband that begins with "Dear Senior Citizen," he will lose a vote. Yet another office seeker is going to stop those rascally harassing phone calls and protect my privacy. It's an election year, and we're all on the yellow trick road to Utopia. Of course, it's worth remembering that Utopia, translated, means no place. Still, I'll long remember that evening at a candidates'meeting when I felt ever so loved. Besides, I came away a better-informed voter, and if I don't vote, I lose the only power I have as a participating citizen in a representative democracy.

Rural Aging

West Virginia hosted the first international aging conference that focused on rural aging, although I'm not sure how those of us in the country age differently from those of you in the city. Maybe our lungs are pinker in the winter of our lives—maybe. Anyway, it's little wonder that West Virginia was chosen as host for the conference. According to all reports, the state now has moved ahead of Florida—that mecca for old people—in the number of, uh, senior citizens living here. The reports prior to the old-folks census claimed we had more fat people, more heart attacks, and more users of snuff and chewing tobacco than any other state. Despite all those frightening statistics, West Virginians do live to grow old and be called "senior citizens." The word "old" long ago collected so many negative connotations hanging from its sagging sides that "old" had to be replaced with senior. But, heck, where are the junior citizens or the freshman citizens? I've never heard anything about junior citizen centers or junior citizen discounts. We don't hesitate to call a young person, well, a young person. That's a telling fact about the way we really feel about old folks, all conferences aside.

If you read the obituaries (and I try not to do that too often), you might see what our neighbor has noticed. First, most West Virginians do die in their old age, and, second, as our astute neighbor told us, they die in alphabetical order. Do you think other states are that organized?

I wasn't asked to speak at the conference on aging, but someone like me would have been far more representative of the rural aging person than someone like Hugh Downs, Geraldine Ferraro, or Willard Scott, the featured speakers. I'm sure they're all wonderful people and excellent orators who, no doubt, age properly. Still, they are hardly typical old folks in West Virginia—or anywhere else, for that matter. In fact, they are celebrities frequently surrounded by adoring fans. Moreover, they are wealthy, a fact that permits them to have various body parts lifted and tucked and stapled. We viewers get the mistaken notion we should look as young as they since they may be about the same age as we. Wealthy persons can have hair removed in one place and replaced in another. When a renowned doctor examines them, he or she is careful to use euphemisms when dictating data into tiny palm-held recorders about their renowned patients' physical changes. A friend told me that in the past few years during her physical exams her doctor called various parts of her body atrophied. Now, there's a word that's familiar to the typical member of the geriatric gang. Anyway, those speakers at the aging conference couldn't begin to know what the rest of us know about growing old. Since we don't have things fixed and tucked and smoothed, we get the full picture each time we look into the mirror, mirror on the wall.

Since I have reached that senior-citizen stage without benefit of fame and fortune, I have scrutinized every subtle change in my body. What's more, I have noticed the same changes in my aging friends. I'm not counting those women who take estrogen with a little testosterone thrown in for safety's sake. They stay young forever. For the rest of us, we can expect thinner lips and thicker hips. Our wasp waists disappear and are replaced with big bellies, located high or low, depending on our gender. Our eyes get smaller, and our chins double or triple. Our hair gets thinner in one place and then moves to a place it should never be. We can't see things close to our eyes, but we have a faraway vision that's second to none. While our sight is flawed, our insight is awesome. Along with the onset of wrinkles, we've gained a storehouse of knowledge and experience while traveling up and down and over the twisting, rough roads of life. Don't, then, just ask us to play bingo and weave baskets and eat low-cost lunches at one of the numerous senior citizen centers. Rather, hire us or ask us for sage advice. Use us as our country's richest resource, but don't patronize us.

I wonder if a speaker at the conference on aging made any of those statements.

Sad in Winter

It's that time of year again. If you aren't careful during these bleak winter days that are as short as the hairs on my dog's back, you might find yourself suddenly crying at nothing, flying off the proverbial handle, feeling tired, eating all the sweets in the house, and even screaming at your spouse or significant other. Whether male or female, you might do all or any combination of these things. You'll be glad to know that if you weep frequently and generally misbehave, you're excused. You see, these winter days—so short that if you blink, you miss daylight altogether—have afflicted you with SAD. Now, you can paradoxically be glad and sad at the same time because scientists have come up with yet another disease loaded with built-in reasons for general nastiness.

We used to be afflicted with cabin fever. Even if that term is outdated, we had the same symptoms then as folks with SAD have now. Instead of getting cabin fever today, we get SAD, an acronym for Seasonal Affective Disorder. Yep, folks, we have yet another behavioral disorder, and it is a valid disorder. Scientists work around the clock, though, to come up with new diseases for which, coincidentally, drug companies come up with new drugs for their treatment. The treatment for SAD is a bit different, according to the experts, although there are probably drugs to help alleviate the symptoms.

In case you have a SAD member in your family, here's one recommended treatment. Try this at home, though, only at great risk to your own safety. As soon as the SAD person's eyes open in the morning (or whenever), blast that person with the brightest light you can find. Then run like the dickens (as my mom would say). This blast of light supposedly makes the weary, dreary person less weary of dreary days that offer insufficient sunlight. The answer is simple. Not enough light? Then, let there be light. I haven't tried this at home and, frankly, would fear for my life if I did.

There are other behavioral disorders for which you might find help. Do you know that even your dog can suffer from one of these newfound maladies? No, seriously. Your faithful friend may have OCD (Obsessive Compulsive Disorder). This is a broad term that can be narrowed for specific identification of the problem. If your dog weeps, screams, and chews your favorite book, excuse the poor thing. It has OCD or, more specifically, Separation Anxiety (SA). The treatment? Don't leave your dog—even for a minute.

At the beginning of one semester when I was teaching at a local college, a colleague told me I had a student with BD. I asked if it was contagious.

She said, "No, Dolly, he has [are you ready?] Behavior Disorder."

Whoa! During the first class with my BD student, he talked more than I did. Disgusted, other students rolled their eyes heavenward. I told him I'd like to speak to him after class. With his hair styled like Katie Couric, he sauntered confidently toward my desk. His brown eyes, like dancing beads, met mine during flickering seconds. I informed him he must refrain from talking in my class. He said he couldn't, that he was a CT, a compulsive talker.

I said, "Then you must drop my class, and I don't know what will happen to you. You can control this if you try. The quality of your life depends on it."

You can see that college professors are not trained to deal with these special education students. I didn't know what else to do, but I did know that I had too many students who would be cheated if this one student couldn't be controlled.

He promised to try. He did. He succeeded. At the beginning of the following year, I saw a newspaper article on the front page of the paper that included a picture of him, smiling brightly. He credited one of his professors for helping him have a first successful year in college. A few days later, I saw him on campus.

He aimed a shy grin my way and said, "You know I was talking about you. Nobody had ever told me to be quiet before."

Certainly, not all behavioral disorders can be taken lightly or handled in the uninformed way I was forced to handle an alleged disorder. Some behavioral problems are quite serious, and those folks need all the help the experts can give them. But if you have cabin fever, er, SAD, don't cry. Just turn on more lights and wait for spring.

Snow Show

During the night when darkness had snuffed out light as only country darkness can, something jarred me awake. Wide-eyed, I sat up in bed, listening. I heard nothing but the usual household noises—a creak here, a hum there. Soon, though, a flash of lightning illuminated the landscape beyond the bedroom window. A rumble of thunder followed. I couldn't believe it, but a thunderstorm and blizzard were occurring simultaneously. The temperature had dipped below freezing, and heavy snow was quickly covering the ground.

Having recently moved from our townhouse with its tiny yard and surrounding concrete to a country cottage with lots of land and wildlife, we had traded a level home site for one on a steep hill.

In that strange night, I turned on the bedside lamp, got up, and walked into the hall. As I entered the kitchen, another thunderclap jarred the house. The lamp went out, the hum of the refrigerator ceased, the green numbers on the microwave disappeared, and the furnace stopped, just stopped. Thrust into silent gloom, I knew the house would soon be cold. Looking toward our daughter's house, I saw nothing but a black velvet void. Our son's house was lost to darkness as well.

As the faint gray of daylight approached, we saw the snow had not abated. Within the next few days, hovering around a gas fireplace my husband had recently installed, we discovered what family togetherness meant. Our son, his wife, our daughter, her husband, and their young son all gathered with us around the tiny fire in our basement—a place my husband insists I call "the lower quarters." By the fourth day, nerves were shattered. We wanted hot food, showers, and warmth.

Our daughter, one of several family wits, said to her husband, "Don, if you would rate our hair on a scale of one to ten how would you rate Mom's, Pam's, and mine?"

I remember he gave me a five, saying my hair looked the way it always had. By the fifth day, though, our humor was sagging like our garage roof under the weight of heavy snow. Our son and son-in-law climbed to the roof, and when they finished shoveling snow to the ground, they no longer needed a ladder to descend. They just stepped from the roof onto the piles of snow they had removed.

My husband and I still owned our empty townhouse, so we decided to go to the city where we could wash clothes and bodies. We would have stayed at the townhouse until power was restored, but in the country we had pets and water pipes to protect, so it would be a quick, efficient roundtrip. Our private country road (about a thousand feet long) was impassable by vehicle. Even walking was difficult. Carrying something heavy while walking was impossible. Our daughter placed her three-year-old son on a piece of plastic at the top of her driveway and gave him a gentle push. Zooming through the rutted-out snow trench, he landed safely at the bottom where his father awaited him.

We crammed our clean clothes into large black garbage bags and courageously high-stepped through deep snow, dragging our makeshift garment bags behind us. We managed to get to Don's truck. Several rode in the back as he drove off the hill on a road that had been cleared by the highway department, but we knew it wouldn't stay clear long. Our cars were parked at the bottom, so the rest of the trip was first-class.

Still teaching, I spent one night in the city so I could get to work. On the seventh and last day without electricity in the country, I answered the phone at the townhouse. I learned my husband had fallen at the top of the hill. His patella tendon had come loose, leaving the kneecap free to travel upward to his thigh. Unable to stand, he made a sled of his body and slid on his back to the foot of the hill where he crawled to the door of a neighbor's house. No one was at home, and he was beginning to freeze. Alone, he lay helplessly beside the road. State road workers drove past and rescued him. I told him if he had just stayed out there another day, I could have written about his experience and sold the piece to Reader's Digest. He didn't smile.

This story has a moral. If you see lightning and snow at the same time, beware. As Ray Bradbury might say, something wicked is coming your way.

Spring for Love

In the blue mist of early morning, faint outlines of huge birds moved about like ghosts from the Mesozoic Era. As the haze lifted, I was startled to see through the window gigantic fowl eating in our front yard. I had never seen such animals.

"Bill, come here! Flying dinosaurs have landed! Hurry!" I yelled.

I had just seen Jurassic Park and still felt a chill when I thought about some scientist's discovery of the makings of a dinosaur egg preserved in mysterious amber. My husband assured me the creatures were nothing more exotic than wild turkeys.

Since then, I've had several opportunities to observe these magnificent birds, including one chance to watch a mating ritual in the spring when a young tom's fancy turns to love. Ah, springtime!

My first up-close and personal view of a male turkey was astonishing in its revelations. He was as handsome as any creature I had ever seen, and he seemed to know it. Recently, on the doorstep of spring, I marveled at his beauty. He strutted across our front yard, king of his domain. At first I thought his feathers were copper-colored, but as he turned under the bright sun, his colors changed as rapidly as those in a rotating kaleidoscope. Each time he changed positions, his feathers became a coat of other colors. They evolved from copper to verdigris—that old-world greenish blue, a color that usually veneers aged brass or copper. As he turned this way and that, his coat continued to change, but always it glistened and glimmered like an animated jewel in the spring sunlight.

He swaggered around our house to the backyard where a flock of feathered females contentedly ate lunch. I thought he was much more handsome than they were beautiful, but they cared not. Ignoring him, they behaved as if he didn't exist. His fancy had nonetheless already turned to love. It was spring after all. He puffed up his feathers and began his courting ritual. Close to the ground, his head jutted forward. With his neck forming a sideways S and feathers fluffed, he sneaked up behind a young lady who had caught his eye. With turkey-sharp vision, she saw him and immediately ran away. He stayed in hot pursuit for a short time, then must have thought to heck with it, for he stopped and ate a bit of lunch. He dined only a few minutes, though, when thoughts of love intruded again and off he went, pursuing the target of his desire. His heartthrob turned and looked at him with disdain and said something I could not hear from my vantage point. My guess is that she told him she had a headache because she was having no part of Handsome Thomas. There's no explanation for the poor taste of some young women. I thought he was the best looking one in the yard. Frankly, those mediocre ladies could have done a lot worse, but if they're anything like some young women, they'll probably wait for something worse to come along.

Male doves fare no better than Mr. Tom. In the vernal season when the male doves spring for love, the females run away so fast on spindly legs they form a gray blur. The lady dove apparently offers the same lame headache excuse. As James Thurber says in his "Courtship Through the Ages," it is always so with the female, regardless of species. Thurber was right. The female isn't as excited about spring love as the male, generally speaking, you understand. I do know about exceptions.

Many theories exist to explain the extinction of the dinosaur. I have one, too. The female dinosaurs all had a collective colossal headache and ran away. The males couldn't catch them and never tried again.

Whether it's doves, turkeys, or humans, the male pursues and the female resists. So, fellows, when Cupid strikes this spring, just candy and flowers will not suffice. Why, they will be no more enticing than Mr. Turkey's beautiful coat of many colors. You'll also need a good pair of running shoes, and if you've already mated for life, offer an aspirin.

Taking the Wind out of Sales

"Ms. Winthrow, this is Marsha. How ya doin' today?" The woman whose voice came over the phone line had an accent that was definitely not Appalachian. It was also clear she was not familiar with the Withrow name. She told me I was one of the chosen few to receive a free set of recipe books for my kitchen. When I told her we were converting our kitchen into a library and would henceforth be eating out, she thanked me and hung up. Touché! My husband responds to telemarketers by pretending to sell cemetery lots to them (unless the caller is also trying to sell plots). Then, he asks the caller if people can be buried standing up. That's when he gets a quick "thank you, have a nice day, goodbye." There are soft- and hard-sell strategies out there. But there's one no one mentions: the sneaky sales pitch.

When you get an invitation to a party and think you're getting popular, beware. It might be a friend using the sneaky approach. I've been invited to several such parties and confess have, in turn, invited others to one I was hoodwinked into hosting. Drat, I hate to admit that. One time, I was even called a "groupie" because I attended the same kind of kitchen-gadget party twice with the same salesperson demonstrating all those magical tools; she made us call them tools. She told me I would make a great demonstrator for her company. She had never watched me try to bake cookies that even squirrels couldn't bite. Watching her whip and beat and chop and mix in front of a roomful of hungry partygoers, I knew had I been in her place, I would have had food on every lap in the room.

Young women host lingerie parties. I'm not about to attend one of them because I now have a shape like a 140-pound bag of baking potatoes. I simply couldn't imagine sporting the latest under-wire bra in front of women shaped like drinking straws. A svelte acquaintance of mine says the lingerie parties are lots of fun. I'll bet.

Candle parties stretch things a bit for the salesperson. It's hard to keep up friendly chatter when the sale of candles alone is your sole purpose. There are candles that won't smoke, won't burn as quickly, and will fill a room with an aroma like a cross between gardenias and sour feet. Candlesnuffers come in handy with some scented candles. There are candles to suit every taste. They come in every shape, size, color, aroma, odor, and stench you can imagine. You can see, then, that there is more to talk about when selling candles than I first thought.

Cosmetic parties are popular with women who don't need them. I attended one and remarked that during the day I was a teacher and at night I searched for Mr. Good Jar. Jars of cream were lined around a large dining room table. Each promised a smooth, dewy complexion. Each lied.

From plastic ware to children's clothing to herbs, products are pitched in homes from coast to coast. According to those who attend these sales get-togethers regularly, they are a peck of fun even if they are costly.

Nothing is more costly to the consumer than television commercials that advertise prescription drugs. I understand that prescription drug prices have skyrocketed, in part, because they are advertised on TV. It's a strange sales approach, too, one for which I have no label. We are instructed in these commercials to ask our doctors about the touted drug—unless, of course, we have liver or heart or kidney problems or are gestating. Moreover, the side effects of various drugs might be diarrhea, stomach pain, headaches, dizziness, and on and on. I don't know about your background, but I don't have the medical training to ask my doctor about specific prescription medications, nor do I have any way of knowing whether I have kidney or liver problems. That's the kind of knowledge my doctor would have after having tests run. From telemarketers to television, we're bombarded with sales tactics, but with a little imagination, we can take the wind out of their sales.

Thanksgiving Secret

Shh-h. You are about to learn the best-kept secret of the Pilgrim's first Thanksgiving feast, a secret of great historical significance, so mark it well (but first, a little background).

My dear daughter-in-law, who says she's never baked a two-legged turkey before (that's what she says), has asked immediate families, her husband's and her own, to come to her home for Thanksgiving dinner. Her generous, but innocent, invitation has called to mind the same innocent invitation in 1621 by one Captain Miles Standish, the Pilgrim's leader.

Backing up one year, though, we know that the Pilgrims first sailed to the shores of Plymouth (rock-infested was the earth there) in 1620. There were so many rocks in the hostile soil the Pilgrims soon discovered that their seeds would not even germinate, much less produce a bountiful harvest. What to do? What to do? They didn't know what to do, and during that first cold, harsh winter—in what is now Massachusetts—many Pilgrims perished.

During the spring of 1621, two American Indians, Squanto and Samoset, were hunting for food near the Pilgrims' settlement. They observed the settlers for several days and agreed the newcomers needed help or they surely would not survive. Squanto had learned to speak English several years earlier when he traveled to England with an English explorer. The two men approached the Pilgrims and soon were teaching the settlers how to grow corn, how to fertilize the soil, and how to conduct many other survival activities. Because of the American Indians' concern and care, the Pilgrims' gardens grew and by fall their harvest provided sufficient food to see them through the following winter.

Being a splinter group of the Puritans, the Pilgrims had built a church of logs and were ready to give thanks for their first harvest in the New World. They had given thanks in England during autumns and would continue the tradition. Likewise, the American Indians had also traditionally given thanks for their good fortune, but their celebration of thanksgiving occurred several times during each year. Regardless of time or religion, then, most of the world's people have a long tradition of giving thanks for good fortune.

Be patient. You're about to learn the secret of the Pilgrim's first Thanksgiving feast in the New World. Captain Miles Standish, wanting to show his appreciation to Squanto and Samoset for helping the Pilgrims to survive, invited them, Massasoit, and the immediate families of the three men to come join the Pilgrims at their Thanksgiving feast. It was a naive invitation because little did the captain know about the size of immediate families in the Indian villages. Of course, there could also have been a misinterpretation of the word "immediate." At any rate, the time came for the grand feast. The Pilgrim women had worked hard to prepare the meal. Large tables were set outside and laden with food.

The American Indians started arriving in much the same way family members begin arriving for Thanksgiving feasts throughout America today. The first few appeared, walking out of the nearby forest. Not given to frivolity, the Pilgrim women, we can imagine, offered tight smiles of welcome. What happened to their smiles during the next hour or so we can also only imagine, for more and more guests appeared. They kept coming and coming and coming in ever greater numbers. The women, along with the inviter, Miles Standish, had to be getting as nervous as the wild turkeys in my yard during hunting season. According to various records, by the time all the members of the three immediate families had arrived, they numbered close to a hundred. Add that to the number of Pilgrims, and you can see the hosts had a multitude to feed. Actually, the men and women who had been invited to share in the Pilgrims' bounty could readily see there was not enough food for everyone. Samasoit came to the rescue. A leader among his people, he ordered his men to go back to the village and bring more food. Now, here's the secret I've promised to reveal. As I see it, Samasoit and Miles Standish were the forerunners of the covered-dish dinner. As far as I know, this was a first in our country. Today, throughout the United States, it is customary for guests to bring covered dishes to supplement the meal, whether it's a back-yard picnic or a holiday dinner.

The American Indians joined in the great feast in 1621, one to which they had greatly contributed. The mixing of different cultures and religions during that time demonstrated that multiculturalism existed even before the United States became a nation. There have been continual attempts to bring people of diverse backgrounds together in peace and harmony. A little more than a hundred years ago, in 1898, the Federal government declared that Thanksgiving would become a national holiday to be observed on the last Thursday of each November. During those quiet few moments before the feast begins in most homes throughout the land, we each in our own way give thanks for a free nation and its bounty, for our veterans who have helped to keep our nation free, and (if we know our history) for the Native Americans who helped to ensure the first bountiful feast for a new people in a new place.

The Business of Language

Allergic to meetings, I had already begun to break out in hives, my usual reaction to any kind of meeting. The monthly assemblies, mandated by our legislators, had to be held whether there was anything of merit to discuss or not. By golly, if legislators had to meet, then we professors had to meet, period.

We routinely met, then, despite stacks of ungraded essays, despite students waiting in the halls, despite class agendas to be prepared. We met and met and met. If we had no topics to discuss, there was always the business of language. During one session, we spent hours trying to decide if there was a difference in the terms strategic planning, objective planning, and tactical planning. Probably because we wanted to go back to our offices and work, we finally decided the expressions all merged and meant much the same thing.

During a faculty workshop (another kind of meeting altogether), we spent one hour trying to distinguish between goal and objective. I don't think we had either at the time, but we had to discuss something, for we were, after all, scholars forced to meet.

Now the word scholar is at the top of the most-loved words in higher education. It has been paraded around campuses so much that it's grown ragged around the edges, weary, tired, trite. Redundancy sometimes has merit all its own. Still, we were scholars, so we met and discussed goals and objectives. During an especially scholarly session, we English faculty even discussed deconstruction. Don't worry if you don't know what that means; you'll live a whole lifetime without it. While scholar is at the top of the professors' love-that-word list, faculty development is at the top of the administrators' list of favorite terms. Actually, it's a phrase that really means getting the faculty to work more for less.

The terminal degree, on one level, means the doctoral degree; on another, it means the killing-field degree. You're almost terminated while you work on it. You can readily see the connection between doctoral and terminal.

The most troublesome part of any new job, though—whether it's in education industry, business, or government—is the ubiquitous use of acronyms and initialisms.

During our first departmental meeting, way back when I thought meetings were held for real reasons, I spent most of the meeting time trying to decipher the strange language.

One efficient professor, silhouetted by the setting sun just beyond the window where she slumped wearily in her chair, said, "That item should be referred to the FPC."

I never heard another word during the rest of that meeting. My mind was racing as I tried to figure out what FPC meant. FPC? Faculty Poobah Committee? Friendly Peace Committee? We could use one of those. Naw. You can understand the blockage in communications when these initialisms are tossed about, but they're used constantly. Why, it's little wonder we ever understand one another. When I think about it, I guess we don't. Still, we muddle along. Anyway, as a scholar, I should not use the word use. Instead, I should use utilize, a word that means the same, but it takes more time, space, and letters. Besides, utilize makes me sound, well, scholarly—ditto for utilization instead of use.

When I presented writing workshops in industry, I was peppered with letters that stood for I knew not what: MDA, R&D, UDC, and someone was even a TA (ta-ta?). I asked the participants if they had trouble deciphering the countless acronyms when they were new employees. All of them did, so communication in industry can be as befuddling as it is in education. If something goes BOOM in a chemical industry, we probably can trace the cause to AAOI (an acronym or initialism).

Business, in general, fares no better. These meaningless letters, substituted for understandable words, have crept, like spreading mildew, across the landscape where they obscure meaning.

NAM, RAM, ROBAM, and PISAM are all acronyms (initial names), according to my friend in the business world. He is a TM, and his friend is a DM. Don't ask me for interpretations. My motto is "Don't ask;

don't tell."

I wonder if the Federal Government is the birthplace of letters that spell nothing or spell puzzling words. A small sampling reveals FEMA, FBI, CIA, FDIC, and FHA. Of course, we all know substitute letters in general use. They include KISS, ASAP, FYI, and RSVP. In the meantime, we all think we're communicating with one another. IDTS (I don't think so).

Treasure Hunting

She was a wise librarian, that one, and pretty, too, with beautifully styled white hair. Friendly and willing to be of help—a real asset to the local library—she looked at my husband and asked, "Are you researching your genealogy?"

He hesitated, not quite sure how to explain his real purpose. I came to the rescue. "I'm going to confess something here." said I. "He wants to know where the gold is buried in Goldtown, West Virginia. If you can help him to find that, we'll be most grateful."

Obviously taken aback, she hesitated, but only for a few seconds. With a sly grin, she asked, "Will you cut me in on the gold?"

"Absolutely," we answered in unison. One will promise anything to get the gold.

Memories of the movie *Adventures of Sierre Madre* and its treasure of gold drifted over the backroads of my mind. I could see the three of us, glinty-eyed, sitting around a campfire, each of us wondering how we could dispose of the others, thereby getting all the gold.

The desire to find treasure is buried deep within the human heart. Most only dream of treasure hunting, but my husband has invested in a metal detector. He has taken action. He reads and digs and plots and plans.

As I watch him walking about our yard, swinging his metal detector in a wide arc, I hear it whistle and beep, giving the message, "Whoa! Treasure here!" I've discovered that these detectors lie. They whistle "treasure" when any kind of metal lies hidden in the ground. Now, if we can just find a market for those tabs on the top of pop cans, we'll be wealthy beyond our mildest dreams. Despite these failures, my husband has found real treasure in his persistent quest.

His in-depth research has revealed some worthwhile knowledge, perhaps the best kind of treasure. During the Civil War, the only thoroughfare from Charleston to Parkersburg was little more than a wide path, which is now Route 21. As everyone knows, part of West Virginia's people supported the North, and part supported the South. Often even family members were divided. Soldiers, then, could steal and plunder their neighbors' belongings if their neighbors were the enemies. Banks were not to be trusted. All this means that most stolen property had to be buried. West Virginia's hills must surely be laden with treasures.

What's more, my husband was told that Goldtown got its name because of an attempt to mine gold somewhere—where, oh, where?—in the town. Actually, we've had trouble finding Goldtown itself, although I'm told we live in it, despite our Kenna address. I'm not sure where its boundaries are, which might cause a bit of a problem when we're trying to find the mother lode. West Virginia's Silverton acquired its name because silver is said to have been mined there. According to various accounts, our state definitely has a silver lining, with silver deposits having been reported in several counties.

Most treasure seekers, though, do not dig in the good earth for their rare finds. Rather, they look for gems at roadside flea markets, yard sales, or in musty buildings that house both junk and gems. Our daughter, like her father, loves to look for hidden treasures. She is a frequent shopper at roadside markets, estate sales, and junk shops. One such local shop is rich in history, for it was at one time an old train station. Just a few examples to be found in these places include bookcases, lunch boxes, toys, cupboards, antique watering cans, tables, chairs, and even church pews.

Looking for instant wealth has become a national pastime. Lotteries are springing up all over the country; many folks now stand in long lines in the hopes of winning the big one. Despite their minuscule chances, they never give up. Others play the stock market. These young investors who didn't live through the Great Depression have made a great deal of money. Of course, it could be ephemeral; it could vanish as quickly as the smoke from that imaginary campfire around which the librarian, my husband, and I continue to plot and dream.

As I watch my husband swinging his metal detector back and forth, though, I know his real thoughts. He has shared them with me. The real treasure, he has said, lies in the anticipation, in the hunt itself.

Up a Tree Without a Paddle

Soon, we Americans will not be able to walk to the malls to buy more plastic toys for our children and grandchildren lest we get swept along in a tide of glassy-eyed marchers. They're everywhere. At one time or another, they're in the nation's capital or on Main Street, USA. They're in virtually every neighborhood and outside every state capitol. We have the million-man march, the million-dad march, and the million-mom march. You name it; we have it. We have protesters for and against just about anything you can imagine. I don't know how we have time to work or, for that matter, to play either. We're too busy protesting and answering those who protest against us. A note is in order about those million-something marches. There are never a million marchers in any given protest. That's just a nice round number promoters use to impress the four or five of us not engaged in another march at the time.

One group about which I read recently even protested the freedom of domestic cats. They chanted, "Put them on leashes. Put them on leashes." I spoke with Elizabeth Tailless, my cat, about this, and before I knew it, she was lying on her back with her two front paws across her ample belly. She laughed uproariously. She informed me that cats have been worshipped along Cleopatra's Nile. They have been burned at the stake in Hawthorne's Salem. She told me her ancestors have even been buried alive to protect crops and added that the foolishness of humans throughout cat history has never ceased to amaze her. Never, however, since thousands of years B.C., has anyone been able to contain or control a cat for any period of time. Cats are so independent they don't even associate with their own kind. They've been called gods and kings and queens and witches and soothsayers, but they've not been held captive for long, said my Elizabeth.

Of course, demonstrators do not confine themselves to petty catty problems, nor do they confine themselves to cities. Protesters creep into dark forests and climb steep mountains. One dedicated woman found herself up a tree and out on a limb where she remained for such a long period of time that food and water had to be transported to her via a pulley. I'm not sure how she disposed of the food and water once it had been ingested, but that would be material for another protest—perhaps. Mother Nature's single bolt of lightning could have brought that huge redwood to the ground in a split second, but she withheld lightning, and the woman did save the tree.

We've never been in a time of greater prosperity. Most of us Americans are overfed and over-pampered, all of which gives us time to worry about cats and leashes, about where we're going to store one more CD or PlayStation or plastic thingamajig. We've become a nation with an attitude.

We're left to wonder what the Pilgrims would have done had they embraced our protester mentality. Certainly, they came to our shores out of protest, but they were of one mind. They were not splintered into opposing factions, divided. Had the Pilgrims formed two sides, one demonstrating against the other, we would be, as my mom would say, up a tree without a paddle.

Weather Bored

"Fords recalled." That was the lead into a make-believe television program on an old Bob Newhart sit-com. George, the host of the show within a show, wanted to lure more viewers to his program. He came up with the advertising blurb "Fords recalled." It worked. Folks gathered around their television sets in record numbers, watching to see if their cars were being recalled. What they saw was a lineup of guests discussing recollections of their first Fords.

Facing increasing competition, television executives are trying the same tack in an effort to attract more viewers. Only the warnings are not supposed to be make-believe. The hype of Y2K is a typical example. The predictions of computer glitches and terrorist bombings were not supposed to be make-believe, but you never know. Of course, the economy received a good boost. We shoppers stood in long lines behind carts piled high with bottled water, batteries, bread, and other provisions. In retrospect, it was a silly thing to do, but we just couldn't help ourselves. We reasoned it was better to be prepared, just in case the experts knew what they were doing. Silly, silly us (I couldn't bring myself to write, "silly we").

Like George's car recall, though, frightful predictions work. We are lured into watching the news every day, lest we miss a warning and perish due to lack of knowledge. If Y2K prophecies weren't enough to scare us out of our proverbial wits, then weather forecasts might do the job—that is, when we can understand them.

Even the titles of local weather teams have a threatening ring to them: Storm Team, Storm Tracker, and First Warning. A past governor may be the forerunner of such ominous weather language. Several years ago, as governor, Jay Rockefeller issued dire warnings of an oncoming blizzard. He told radio listeners to stay inside and take care of the old folks. I don't believe the term senior citizen had come on the scene yet. Anyway, both young and old were scared. Trying to beat others to grocery stores where every last loaf of bread would disappear from shelves, wild-eyed drivers zoomed up and down highways, their tires screeching and horns blowing. Waiting for the blizzard, I remember looking out the window. The sun had come out, and it stayed and stayed for the whole day and the next. The blizzard never materialized. Soon, people began to joke about Jay's blizzard, but I was told it was more than a year before Rockefeller could even smile about it. We must remember, though, that he received his information from meteorologists. I don't know whether they had Doppler to help them then or not.

Technology has moved with a vengeance onto the weather forecasting scene. After a couple of TV anchors and the sports commentator chat with one another about the weather—ignoring us viewers completely—they finally turn to the expert. He or she stands in front of a map of the United States. We can see fronts move across the map. Clouds roll over outlines of unlabeled states so most of us are not sure which states are which, but the clouds roll onward. Snow and rain and sun take on an electronic life, right there on the TV screen. We watch. Alberta clips her way down from Canada, bringing frigid air over the northern and western states. We wait and wait for the local forecast. We're told of cold fronts and warm fronts. Vertical air masses and slanting air masses are all over the place. A low-pressure system's here, and a high-pressure system's there. The wind is steady at 14 mph, and the barometer is 29.7, also steady. The old Doppler shows another cold front coming our way. Phew! I tell you it's more than we need. We just want to know whether the weather is going to cause us to carry an umbrella, shovel snow, or wear sunglasses. That and the temperature would be sufficient.

Aside from lengthy weather discussions, our evening news is filled with warnings of food contamination, hospital mistakes, bomb threats, and car recalls. You'll want to watch to see if your car is being recalled.

Which Witch?

Long, long ago in Scotland, a witch was known as a weird person. Indeed, the word "weird" was a pseudonym for "witch." You remember the three weird sisters in Shakespeare's *Macbeth*. They are actually witches, and when they chant, "Fair is foul, and foul is fair," they tell us something about the philosophy of those witches who couldn't distinguish between foul and fair. I suppose today we have added an "o" to "weird," thereby transforming the adjective "weird" into the noun "weirdo." My point is that if weirdos are still witches, then we have a larger number of witches among us than we ever imagined. Of course, there are wicked witches from the West, I think, and good witches from somewhere else. Our job is to figure out which witch is which witch.

Wicca was the name for a male witch in Old English, a language not to be confused with today's American Standard English, which is as foreign to most folks as Old English anyway.

I'm not about to ridicule witches, wiccas, or weirdos, lest I have an evil spell cast upon me, and I lose my other eyebrow. No, sir-eee. Why, even a commander in the United States Army with all its artillery and personpower is powerless against wiccas and witches who have demanded and received the right to dance around their bonfires. The good news is that if missiles are headed our way, surely these soldier witches and wiccas can just wiggle their noses and dissolve those nasty missiles. Our Constitution, I was told reluctantly by an Army spokesperson, gives these folks their right to religious freedom. Of course, all such ceremonies, like bonfire dancing, began many centuries ago.

The Celtic calendar's New Year began on November 1, making the last night of October old year's night or the night of all witches. The church changed the name of the eve to All Saints' Eve or All Hallows' Eve. You can see the short broom-hop from All Hallows' Eve to Halloween. In the British Isles, the Celts built huge bonfires, and roaming groups of children in scary costumes carried lanterns made of carved turnips. This was long before turnip trucks, so we can't say someone fell off the turnip truck and then began chanting around a bonfire.

The Druids, those ancient priests, held a celebration from November

1-3, lighting bonfires to frighten away the spirits of the dead, which they believed roamed the earth in the dark of night on October 31. All Hallows' Eve was also a night when costumed children went from door to door begging for treats. The giving of these treats would ensure a good year for the giver.

It's almost here again, that night when witches, wiccas, gremlins, and grammarians strut their stuff—that is, if grammarians are still considered sorcerers or witches as they were during medieval times. In fact, during the dark ages, people feared grammarians. Even the grammarians' apprentices became so addled trying to learn the complicated rules of grammar that they gave it up altogether. There were then a diminishing number of this special type of sorcerer until today we have only a small handful in the entire country. They are still feared and pretty much ignored. To understate the case, grammarians are not popular as they wield their pens with blood-red ink, scarring papers from top to bottom. I've never seen a grammarian ride a broom, and I've never ridden one, but you never know.

Am I above all this seeming foolishness? Not at all. When I was a child, I dressed in adult clothes, painted my face with makeup, and joined my friends to go trick or treating. We often walked about a mile from our homes on Brickyard Hill to the USO (now the North Charleston Recreation Center), where a huge bonfire shot flames toward the dark October sky. I didn't know it then, but centuries before, children had gone through the same rituals.

As a child, I knew no more of the history of Halloween than most children know today. They are just children experiencing the magic of childhood on the one night they can be anyone or anything they want to be. When I see tiny characters like witches, ballerinas, and Power Rangers coming to my door, I reach for the bowl of candy and willingly share. When costumed adults, not accompanied by children, come to our door and ask for treats, my husband hits the inside of their trick-or-treat bags with his hand but drops nothing in them. The begging adults say, "Thank you." As I watch them walk down the walk away from our house, I know there are all sorts of tricks played on that most playful of all nights, Halloween.

Who Wants to Marry a Richard Gere Clone?

Did you hear the sounds of Western civilization crumbling as two strangers were married for viewers' entertainment on "Who Wants to Marry a Multimillionaire," the Fox television program? A sociologist declared that such sounds could be heard, and little wonder. The show attracted almost 23 million viewers in its final segment. That's called the bottom line, but Fox has outfoxed itself. Astute observers, like the sociologist, must conclude that millions of Americans have become devoted viewers of degrading shows. They spring for Jerry Springer and just adore Jenny Jones. At the same time, they love to denounce the very shows they support by watching them each week. I know viewers who criticized the Multimillionaire program and especially condemned the 50 women who were chosen from thousands of eager applicants willing to marry a wealthy stranger— sight unseen. The fifty women (who have been called a number of other names) were reduced to ten, but the final cut left only five. They wore bathing suits and paraded around the stage in Miss America fashion. I did not watch the show, but reruns of segments and news accounts have informed every conscious person of every detail. The five competitors answered questions from one rich Rick Rockwell, who was hidden behind a curtain as he viewed the women vying to be his chosen bride.

According to widespread news reports, much of his past was also hidden. An actor and comic, he at one time had a minor role in a movie titled *Killer Tomatoes Strike Back*. We'll not make too much of that, but he was also issued a restraining order from a former fiancee who said he had physically abused her. More recently, we have learned that a former male friend was threatened, and that he, too, had to initiate a restraining order against Mr. Multimillionaire. Well, well.

Seeing a rerun segment of the show, I watched four pitiful would-be brides slowly turn their backs to the camera and slink off the stage— their heads lowered and long white tails of bridal gowns dragging behind them. Talk about being all dressed up and no one to marry. Bet those rejected brides-to-be are now privately celebrating somewhere, realizing how close they came to being in Darva Conger's white satin shoes. In all fairness to rich Rick (we think he's rich but aren't sure now), he told Darva it was unfair for him to get to ask all the questions. I'll say.

Darva, you may recall, is the woman who just wanted to get out of the emergency room at the hospital where she made lots of her own money, thank you. She just wanted a paid vacation and then wanted to return to her normal life. She never dreamed she would be the chosen one. After the flash-in-the-pan romance of about 30 seconds when rich Rick went down on one knee and proposed, the two were married. That's what some would call cutting to the chase. Of course, we all knew it wouldn't last. It didn't, not even until they left the stage. Darva didn't feel, uh, the chemistry and was appalled at the sloppy kiss Rick planted on her. She thought he should have just kissed her on the cheek, but, hey, he was her husband by that time. The $35,000 diamond ring and the Isuzu are all that remain with Darva as tender reminders of what she calls one bad judgment.

The show, a brainchild of Mike Darnell at Fox, was a darn foxy idea that didn't quite fly. Darnell, I'm sure, is looking for other ideas, and I have one. If scientists can clone a sheep named Dolly, it won't be long before they can clone a Richard Gere or a Meryl Streep or your favorite celebrity. Then Darnell can create another show with no class. He can title it "Who Wants to Marry a (you fill in the blank) Clone?" Do you hear it— the shattering of our civilization?

Wireless and Clueless

We have e-mail, voice mail, US mail, and cell phones. We have overnight and over the fence. From graffiti to grapevine, from telephone to telepathy to talk radio, from pagers to palm-held computers, we now have more ways of communicating with one another than ever before in the history of humankind. If there was ever a wired generation, we're it. Despite all these wonders, there is a problem. We don't have anything to say.

A rapid movement toward an increased number of technological gadgets that will be wireless is now underway. Clueless we'll remain, though, for we still have little to say. This is not the same as saying we wisely remain in a state of golden silence. If you think we can't find messages to exchange, consider e-mail.

A high-powered, fully wired executive of a Fortune 500 company hadn't checked his e-mail for about a month. When he finally responded to "you've got mail," much to his dismay, he had 700 e-mail messages. He called the technology wizard on staff and asked the wizard to delete all the e-mails (unread, of course). He was informed that could not be done; deleting them was against company policy. The executive, who had achieved that lofty position partly because of his insight, knew that if the e-mails were deleted he wouldn't miss much.

Those canned e-mail messages we continually receive serve in much the same way a baby or pet serves to keep us from real communication. In a restaurant, with a baby at center stage, we adults can all look at the baby and coo over its beauty or innocence and, therefore, not be forced to engage in conversation—trivial or meaningful.

Dumb-blond jokes, bright-blond jokes, skits about angels and imps, sad stories with deep lessons about life, adolescent cartoons (slightly off-color and not at all funny), and, of course, the really dirty stuff make up much of the forwarded e-mails. Oh, yes, there are the ever-present warnings about Y2K and computer viruses, along with the chain letter telling you that if you respond within X number of days you'll be prosperous, healthy, and happy. These canned missives combine to make real communication an art relegated to times past. I can't even imagine folks meeting today at an academy to engage in the art of debate or deep conversation, as was the case in Plato's day.

It's so easy to send those mindless e-mails. Just attach or cut and paste something someone else has written and hit the send button. Sending these shop-worn notes is so inviting, so enticing, and almost irresistible. The speed, as well as the convenience of it all, means we don't have to think even enough to string together one original sentence.

Voice mail suffers the same maladies. In the business world voice mails are filled with buzzwords and phrases like "level the playing field," "push the envelope," "just wanted to touch base with you," and the ever-present "bottom line." I often get messages on my answering machine that say, "I don't really have anything to say, just wanted to talk."

U.S. mail carriers are laden with loads of heavy mail, but their burdensome packs bulge with bills and advertisements. Seldom do we receive beautiful, thought-provoking letters. Of course, at Christmas, we can count on at least three or four generic letters (one size fits all) from friends who want to tell us how much they have achieved, earned, learned––how many promotions, awards, and accolades they and their loved ones have received.

Planes, trains, cars, stores, and restaurants are all places where you can see the ever-present cell phone. My husband and I were in a restaurant recently, and a couple sat in a booth near us. With cell phone to an ear, the man talked loudly, lest we'd miss the fact he was with it, fully wired. His companion played with the remaining food on her plate as he yelled into the phone, "Yeah, man, good talkin' to ya. No, I didn't have anything to say. Just keepin' in touch."

A television was on overhead, placed there by a manager who apparently thought it would increase trade. A soap opera was underway, and we diners could see the actors' lips move but could hear no dialogue. That's the way with all restaurant televisions, but it's okay. We're not missing anything anyway; it's all just a showing off of the sound and fury of communication technology, signifying nothing. *Seinfield*, one of the most popular TV series ever aired, was, according to its own characters, a show about nothing. People loved it.

Several years ago, a man wrote an essay, titled "How to Say Nothing in Five Hundred Words." He was really on to something. As prophetic as Cassandra, his essay was surely a foreshadowing of the future, which is here. Now, I must cut and paste that canned e-mail to all my friends.

Writers and Bellwether Sheep

We writers are a lot like sheep, especially bellwether sheep. You may remember the story about a single sheep that rambled over hill and dale and through the deep woods. In time, it was followed by other bellwether sheep (imitating is their nature, even as it is ours) until at last a crooked path emerged. Other animals traveled the twisting, turning path until, at last, humans (bringing up the rear) made of the path a giant, albeit crooked, highway. Now we writers often follow other writers over torturous, winding paths into dark, confusing forests, and sometimes even over symbolic cliffs.

One writer, for example, will read about a study that indicates a possible fact, but the fact may just as well not be fact, if you're still with me. The fact that the fact may not be fact doesn't deter the bellwether journalist whose nature is to follow.

Take global warming. Most writers—wanting to appear up-to-date and, above all, intellectual and, even beyond that, environmentally savvy—have climbed aboard the global-warning bandwagon. Most writers tell us that an apocalypse is imminent—that is, if we don't stop emitting those bad gases into the air, gases like carbon dioxide and methane, we're headed for disaster. If we don't park our gas-guzzling, road-hog SUVs and get rid of our air-conditioners and get back to nature, we're doomed. If we don't stop cutting trees and mining coal and enjoying the good life in general, the world will surely end, so repeat the bellwether writers. Scientists, however, are not at all in agreement that we're punching holes in the ozone layer, which writers tell us is already as hole-riddled as baby Swiss. Not all scientists believe that if we don't change our way of living we're going to burn to a crisp or have another ice age (depending on which scientist's study we read). Many scientists do not believe the ocean's level will rise and the polar ice caps will melt. Still, that's what we read again and again.

We have been told to plant trees, not cut them. People in Japan probably do this, for they have few trees. In West Virginia, though, we have so many trees that our state could have as appropriately been named The Tree State. Everything is relevant. Anyone who has ever tried to wrestle one-on-one with Mother Nature knows who's going to win. Think multiflora rose or weeds or insects, especially, think ladybug. No person, from the dullard to the scholar, has ever emerged as the victor when battling nature.

Interpretations—like those ever-present studies—change with the times. When I was attending school, my friends and I had never heard the phrase "separation of church and state." We prayed at the beginning of each school day, saluted the American flag, sat down, and learned. If there were students of other faiths in the class, they apparently didn't think the less than thirty seconds required to utter "The Lord's Prayer" (even with our slow Southern dialect) significant enough to protest the prayer. At any rate, protesting was not the norm during those innocent days. As a point of fact, the words "separation of church and state" cannot be found anywhere in the First Amendment. It states, "Congress shall make no law respecting an establishment of religion, or prohibiting the free exercise thereof; or abridging the freedom of speech, or of the press, or the right of the people peaceably to assemble, and to petition the Government for redress of grievances." As another point of fact, on the very day the First Amendment was passed, the founding fathers approved a resolution requesting President George Washington to proclaim "a day of public thanksgiving and prayer. . . ." It is a difference in interpretation that has caused the forbidding of prayer in schools. As a matter of fact, Congress itself printed the first English language Bible in 1782 specifically "for use [in public] schools." Congress today begins every session with prayer, and each President, from Washington to our current President, has referred to God and has bowed his head in prayer at the beginning of official ceremonies.

Documents created by our founding fathers have not changed. Only the interpretations by a few have changed, and those few have blazed a long and crooked path followed by many writers until now interpretations are accepted by many as fact.

Yada-Yada-Yada

I don't think he's a cultural icon yet, but using the language of the beautiful people, he's on his way. I heard him say he had detoxified a recent negative experience. I think he had just gone through a nasty divorce, and I suppose if anything needs to have the poison extracted, a divorce is it. The public speaker, a professor at one of the eight Ivy League institutions, made me realize how anemic my own vocabulary had become. So, here's notice to all. I'm going to evolve into a beautiful person, too. If you want to join me, here's what you must know.

Beautiful people don't learn anything. Instead, they internalize information. When the offspring of the verbal trendsetters don't study, the parents say their children are merely academically disengaged.

Also, close observations have revealed some facts about how different classes of people imbibe. The beautiful people—those in the upper socioeconomic ranks—don't drink wine the way a lone alcoholic gulps it down or the way a man with his buddies in a bar drinks beer from a brown bottle while listening to country tunes. Elegant people call themselves "friends of wine," honest. Only they say it in French. They meet in places where there are seldom enough seats, so they stand in clusters, sipping wine ever so delicately. They talk and talk, describing the quality of the vintage beverage. They use words like balance and body and complexity and vintage years. After pouring white or red wine into crystal glasses, they decant it back and forth, aerating the wine, expanding the bouquet, the taste, and, ultimately, the waist. They serve their wine with hors d'oeuvres— a word easier to pronounce than to spell. Be sure, though, to avoid pronouncing the first part the way it's spelled. As you know, hors d'oeuvres is French. When exquisite persons dine, they sprinkle their comfort food with pricey sea salt, after which they might attend a sensitivity training session.

If they are already sensitive enough, they may attend a meeting to try to find themselves. (The problem with being a beautiful person is you may lose yourself from time to time.) If they've found themselves, they might attend another kind of meeting to rid themselves of the past. I know someone who attended such a meeting (I'm not kidding). The participants had to write all their bad experiences on small pieces of paper. Then, they threw those poison-infested paper pieces into a large metal container and set them on fire. They watched all those inner feelings disappear into air. That did it. My friend told me the burdens lifted from his shoulder, and he felt lighter, happier. Do you think this would work for you?

If we're going to imitate the beautiful people, we must be careful to internalize information while, at the same time, avoiding internalization of external conflicts. And when we do something that is clearly wrong, we say we've done something inappropriate—a slippery eel of a word that will keep us in good light.

We no longer need to work through our problems either. Isn't that a relief? Rather, we go through a healing process. Moreover, we don't have to muster courage and get on with our lives after a tragedy. We meet with grief counselors and, eventually, bring the tragedy to a closure. Anyone who's ever lost a loved one knows this is impossible, but that doesn't matter. This language is not supposed to reflect reality. It is supposed to make us feel good.

Business folks have learned to imitate the euphemism huggers. Executives don't discuss problems or obstacles today. They discuss issues. Employees are not hired. Rather, they come aboard or join the team. Companies love the words team and quality. After too many persons have been brought aboard, the company downsizes. No one is fired anymore. There is more business jargon than could be contained in fifty pages: hidden agenda, level playing field, window of opportunity, and yada-yada-yada.

If you've internalized this, you're on your way to becoming a cultural icon, a beautiful person.

About the Author

Dolly Withrow is the author of two previous books: *From the Grove to the Stars* (©1991) and *The Confident Writer* (©1997, Glencoe/McGraw-Hill), a grammar-based writing textbook for college students and writers, in general. A columnist for *The Jackson Herald* and winner of a national writing contest, she has had her works published in national magazines. In 2000, Dolly received the West Virginia Press Association's first-place award for her columns.

A retired English professor, Dolly teaches for the University of Iowa's world-famous Summer Writing Festival and presents writing workshops to employees of Fortune 500 companies and other clients.